T0028254

THE
AFTER
PARTY

THE
AFTER
PARTY

TOWARD BETTER CHRISTIAN POLITICS

CURTIS CHANG AND NANCY FRENCH

Based on the project created by

CURTIS CHANG · DAVID FRENCH · RUSSELL MOORE

ZONDERVAN BOOKS

ZONDERVAN BOOKS

The After Party
Copyright © 2024 by Redeeming Babel

Published in Grand Rapids, Michigan, by Zondervan. Zondervan is a registered trademark of The Zondervan Corporation, L.L.C., a wholly owned subsidiary of HarperCollins Christian Publishing, Inc.

Requests for information should be addressed to customercare@harpercollins.com.

Zondervan titles may be purchased in bulk for educational, business, fundraising, or sales promotional use. For information, please email SpecialMarkets@Zondervan.com.

ISBN 978-0-310-36870-0 (softcover)
ISBN 978-0-310-36873-1 (audio)
ISBN 978-0-310-36872-4 (ebook)

Unless otherwise noted, Scripture quotations are taken from The Holy Bible, New International Version®, NIV®. Copyright © 1973, 1978, 1984, 2011 by Biblica, Inc.® Used by permission of Zondervan. All rights reserved worldwide. www.Zondervan.com. The "NIV" and "New International Version" are trademarks registered in the United States Patent and Trademark Office by Biblica, Inc.®

Scripture quotations marked ESV are taken from the ESV® Bible (The Holy Bible, English Standard Version®). Copyright © 2001 by Crossway, a publishing ministry of Good News Publishers. Used by permission. All rights reserved.

Scripture quotations marked NRSV are taken from the New Revised Standard Version Bible. Copyright © 1989 National Council of the Churches of Christ in the United States of America. Used by permission. All rights reserved.

Any internet addresses (websites, blogs, etc.) and telephone numbers in this book are offered as a resource. They are not intended in any way to be or imply an endorsement by Zondervan, nor does Zondervan vouch for the content of these sites and numbers for the life of this book.

All rights reserved. No part of this publication may be reproduced, stored in a retrieval system, or transmitted in any form or by any means—electronic, mechanical, photocopy, recording, or any other—except for brief quotations in printed reviews, without the prior permission of the publisher.

Cover design: Faceout Studio, Tim Green
Interior design: Denise Froehlich

Printed in the United States of America

24 25 26 27 28 LBC 5 4 3 2 1

CONTENTS

✦ ✦ ✦

INTRODUCTION

A COMPLICATED QUESTION

"Why don't we see Grandma and Grandpa anymore?"

The question hung in the air.

Sean and Emily exchanged that awkward side glance that parents use when each spouse wants the other to answer.

The Harris family, which included two high school girls and another in college, were on vacation in Costa Rica. It was raining, and the five of them were all cooped up together in the rental car. There was nothing to do and they couldn't avoid each other. This combination of boredom and compression can sometimes surface simmering questions that a family normally avoids.

The girls were asking about Sean's parents, Jack and Cindy. The grandparents lived in Oregon, a twelve-hour drive from the Bay Area home of Sean and Emily. While growing up, the girls most often saw their grandparents when Sean and Emily traveled to Jack and Cindy's home to commemorate special events: graduation parties, birthday parties, and holiday parties. But several years ago, in 2020, those trips had suddenly disappeared.

"I miss them," the youngest daughter added softly.

The only sound was the steady patter of the tropical rain on the car roof. Sean finally broke the silence: "Well, girls . . . um . . . it's complicated."

Then he stopped. Partly, Sean was stalling for time. But it was also the truth: for both him and Emily, it *was* complicated, very complicated.

A simplistic answer that Sean could have offered would have been "Political differences." This answer would have conveyed a grain of truth. Jack and Cindy held conservative political beliefs and Sean and Emily now held views that would be characterized as comparatively more liberal. Such an answer treats political difference as a story of *what*: "What did Sean and Emily believe? What did Jack and Cindy believe? What was the conflict between these two political positions?" Sean could have told the girls this kind of story quickly—and in the process he would have utterly failed to explain the real reasons they no longer saw their grandparents.

Because the fuller story is a more complicated story of *how*: How did everyone involved come to believe what they believed? How did they talk with one another about politics? How did those interactions shape everyone's feelings about one another?

This *how* story more truly explains the disappearing connection within the Harris family and within many American families like them. To understand this more complicated kind of story, one must dig deeper than present-day political positions.

For instance, take the family histories of Jack and Cindy. Both come from families who lived for generations in small towns in Northern California and Oregon where almost everyone was White, Republican, and conservative Christian. They stayed so completely within this environment that, like fish who know only water, they did not have even a theoretical conception that people could grow up in different racial or political environments. Jack admits, "Looking back, most of our Christian friends were from the conservative side. But at the time, I didn't even know there were [politically] conservative or liberal Christians. I thought we were just Christians. I didn't have much experience with diversity." To this day, Cindy struggles to grasp how this homogeneity affected her, so much so that the concept does not have a place in her vocabulary: "I still don't even know what that word *homogenous* means. Looking for differences wasn't even on my radar."

Sean was raised in this environment and, like his parents, knew of no other kind of world. The family eventually moved from their small town to a suburb of Sacramento. Here, pockets of cultural and political liberalism existed, especially in the community college where Jack taught as a math professor, and also in the local public-school system. Jack sometimes complained about the political correctness at the college, but he couldn't do anything about that. He and Cindy could do something about their kids' education, however. When Sean's oldest brother was in the fourth grade, his parents pulled the boys out of public school and put them into a conservative Christian school.

Sean remembers his father listening regularly to the conservative talk-show host Rush Limbaugh. Over family dinners, Jack would rehearse Limbaugh's latest takes on taxes, foreign policy, and the Clintons. Sean and his brothers would eat while listening, nodding in agreement. Jack admits that he didn't have time for other news programs, so there were no other regular sources of information influencing these family discussions.

Sean deeply respected and trusted his father. He sought his father's acceptance. Like many children, he sensed that gaining this acceptance meant agreeing with what his father believed. "Who my dad was, who we were as his sons, and who we were as a Christian family," says Sean, "was bound up in what our shared politics were."

Sean left home for college, attending Cal Poly. At this large state university, he was suddenly confronted with the diversity that composes the entire state of California. Sean joined the InterVarsity Christian Fellowship campus group and for the first time befriended fellow believers who held very different political views from his. On a summer service project in Mexico, he met faithful Christians with entirely different cultural perspectives from his own.

During college, Sean didn't necessarily change his own politics. His father's views were still imprinted on him from those years of dinnertime conversations. But his assumption that Christian identity should equate to conservative politics was weakening.

Accelerating this shift was his relationship with Emily, a fellow member of the Christian fellowship. Emily was a fourth-generation Japanese American with a long family history in California. In 1942, Emily's grandparents were rounded up from their family farm and imprisoned in a concentration camp in Amache, Colorado. Emily's mom was born surrounded by barbed wire. When her family was finally released, they had lost practically everything and had to start over as farmworkers. This history instilled in Emily a keen sympathy with those who have been excluded by our country and a sensitivity to the legacy of systemic injustice.

In 1997, Sean and Emily got married and moved to the Bay Area. Sean started as an engineer in Silicon Valley. Emily began working as a public-school teacher, then a school counselor, where she pursued her passion to reform educational practices that disproportionately hurt immigrant Latino students. Sean and Emily were active in their local evangelical church and were raising three daughters. Emily was the main organizer of the family schedule, and she made sure that, even with the typical busyness of a young family, they made regular trips to visit Sean's family. Emily's side of the family lived nearby in the Bay Area, and it was important to Emily that the girls grew up knowing both sets of their grandparents.

Emily especially grew in her affection for Jack, in particular his virtues of integrity and earnestness. But her appreciation of his character ran into painful experiences with his political views. On one visit in the aftermath of 9/11, Jack read an email that was circulating through the Harris family about the threat of Muslim terrorists in the US. "We need to keep a better eye on them," he read. "We shouldn't be afraid to gather them up in one place if we need to. We've done it before as a country, like we did with the Japanese." Emily stared at him in disbelief, unsure if he had just forgotten about her family history or, worse, if he hadn't. She quickly excused herself, ran to the upstairs bathroom, and sobbed.

After she returned home, she composed an eight-page letter to Jack and Cindy, explaining why the experience was so painful. Jack responded by calling Emily and leaving on her voicemail a heartfelt message of apology.

But the pattern persisted. Emily would visit Sean's parents, and within a day or two the family conversation would turn to politics and she would hear some viewpoint expressed that seemed to ignore her reality as the only non-White and non-conservative member of the family. She tried to convey to them that their limited family time would be better spent talking about what was happening in their kids' or their own personal lives. Jack admitted to her that, temperamentally, he was much more comfortable talking about issues than connecting on emotionally intimate matters—and for him, this meant talking about political issues. Looking back, Jack also recognizes that he wasn't adept at picking up emotional cues. He admits with an admirable level of humility: "I'm not a very good listener—it's something I know I need to work on, but I'm still not very good at it."

Jack tried to adjust. Emily would experience a brief trend where family conversations would steer clear of politics, only for the painful dynamic inevitably to resume. Emily struggled to make sense of it all. Was Jack just unable to realize when he was straying back into the very territory that was most emotionally comfortable for him—and most emotionally threatening to Emily? Or perhaps, as she feared, was Jack actually far more committed to his politics than to her as a person?

Her fears extended to the other members of the Harris family. At a family gathering in Sacramento, one of Sean's brothers complained to Emily about immigrants needing special treatment from schools. "If they don't want to work hard, we should just let them fail," he said. Emily interpreted that as a personal attack on her life's calling and decided she needed to protect herself emotionally. By 2018, Emily determined not to make any more trips to visit Jack and Cindy.

She and Sean tried to shield their daughters from the painful conflict. Sean took the girls on a few trips by himself. Yet the dinnertime conversations grew more and more tense, and Sean felt that his girls were starting to be included in barbs about liberals. Finally, at the end of one especially tense visit near the 2020 election, Sean snapped at Jack with more force than he can remember ever expressing to his father, "You're always trying to set me straight!"

Sean was not proud of that moment, because he could tell the comment hurt his dad.

"I was at a boiling point, unable to explain all my feelings, which had many layers," Sean later explained. "I think I'm just starting to realize that my dad was engaging in our political conversations from a place of relational security. For him, he was just talking about the issues, and that's it, that's all that was happening. When he would express disdain for a view I held, he was targeting just that view. For me, I was engaging from a place of insecurity. I felt I was being implicitly compared to my brother, who always had my dad's respect. I feared that my changing politics had made me the black sheep of the family. I wasn't sure I was still accepted. I was afraid that he disdained me personally."

After this last exchange, all family visits to Oregon ended. Emily continued to organize the family graduation, birthday, and family parties but did not invite Sean's parents. And they didn't seem to express any desire to visit. The momentum of everyone's lives was taking them farther and farther apart.

Except now, in this rental car in Costa Rica, the daughters were asking the question: "Why don't we see Grandma and Grandpa anymore?"

The Harris story illustrates that the *what* story—of differing ideologies, parties, and policies—fails to adequately answer such a question. For most relationships that have disappeared or are at risk of disappearing, there is a far more important story of *how*. The Harris story is a story of how Cindy's homogenous background ill prepared her for recognizing how others differ from her. It is a story of how Jack feels emotionally safer debating political issues than connecting on a more intimate relational level. It is a story of how Emily's own background makes her especially sensitive to exclusion. It is a story of how Sean is still coming to terms with his complicated family dynamics.

Moving from the simplistic *what* toward the more complicated—and more truthful—*how* story of politics is the purpose of this book. We believe this move is especially critical for Christians to adopt because in Christian families, friendships, and churches we are increasingly disappearing from each other.

REFLECTION EXERCISE

Who has disappeared from your life because of politics?

Perhaps you, too, have experienced complicated feelings around this question. Perhaps you have picked up this book because, for whatever reason, you think it might finally be time to address it.

Do this quick exercise. On a separate piece of paper, write down the people who have disappeared from your life because of political tension.

Here are some prompts:

- Whom do you no longer see at church, either because they've left or you've left?
- Whose texts have you stopped getting because you blocked them for the offensive links that they shared?
- When you go to another city, is there a local friend or family member you no longer try to see because you fear that even a catch-up conversation could turn to current events?
- Who has disappeared from your social media feed because their posts and comments were so disagreeable?
- Which family members have stopped showing up at Thanksgiving or Christmas because of a past conflict or simmering tension about politics?
- Whom have you stopped inviting to your parties? Whose parties are you no longer invited to?

After you've written down your list of names,

review it and think of the people behind those names. What are your feelings? Circle each word that resonates with you, and add any not on this list.

- anger
- sadness
- affection
- guilt
- curiosity
- revulsion
- insecurity

- obsession
- resentment
- confusion
- outrage
- powerlessness
- (fill in the blank)

THE DISAPPEARED ONES

The emotions are complicated, aren't they? They are complicated because behind each name is a complicated individual story. And all of those complicated individual stories contribute to a complicated national story.

Right now, in the United States, we're in the middle of something that journalist Bill Bishop has termed "the Big Sort." Americans are moving to locations or increasingly living in locations where they're surrounded by people who share their same beliefs. We have forgotten how to disagree with our neighbors, because we no longer live near people with whom we disagree. Millions of Americans are now less likely to live near people they disagree with than at any other time in recent memory or since researchers have been tracking this statistic.

Moving to be with people of like mind is not necessarily wrong. Families move from one location to another for myriad reasons. Sometimes it's just easier and more comfortable to live in a place that reflects your values. But ideological isolation comes at a cost, to ourselves and to our society.

Many readers will be able to do this exercise and fill their lists with people who disappeared from their lives because of politics. But some readers may struggle to come up with any names. If that is your case—if all your relationships are as intact as before, untouched by politics—this may mean the Big Sort got to you early. You have been a longtime participant (consciously or unconsciously) in it, which has already made the politically different disappear from your neighborhood, workplace, church, and even extended family. If so, it means you are relatively insulated from the immediate pain experienced by Sean and Emily. But you are even more vulnerable to the kind of long-term dynamics that shaped Jack and Cindy. If diversity was never present in your life, you will struggle to understand others who are different from you and to navigate a national context defined by difference. Homogeneity will make your relationships easier, but it will also make you much more vulnerable to political extremism (and this is true regardless of where you are on the political spectrum). Lilliana Mason, author of *Uncivil Agreement:*

How Politics Became Our Identity, summarizes the research: "A lack of exposure to other ideas and people can make other ideas seem extreme and other people seem totally foreign, even when they are not. This includes both an intolerance of the policy positions of the other side and, more basically, an intolerance of the increasing strangeness of the outsiders. It can make a relatively moderate person intolerant of other views."[1]

We'll further examine this vulnerability later in the book, but the point is this: the people who do not appear in your life still affect you, even if you don't consciously feel the pain of a relational loss.

We are all haunted by the disappeared ones.

The term *the disappeared ones* echoes the political history of another country. Following this echo reminds us that this kind of social disappearance can affect more than just those of us immediately involved; over time and in aggregate, the loss of relationships across political lines can influence the fate of an entire society. In 1970s Argentina, the government's secret police abducted individuals suspected of holding dissident political views. Later investigation revealed many were executed secretly by those security forces. But at the time, no explanation was given for what happened to them or if they might return. The victims became known as *los desaparecidos*: "the disappeared ones."

Americans tend to resist considering how our politics may

---

1. Lilliana Mason, *Uncivil Agreement: How Politics Became Our Identity* (Chicago: University of Chicago Press, 2018), 61–62.

echo the politics of distant countries like Argentina; thus, borrowing a term like *the disappeared ones* for our context can feel dissonant. We think, *Secret police disappearing people? That could never happen here!* And, of course, there is still a large gap between Americans socially separating themselves from political opponents and Argentinians physically eliminating their political opponents.

But a pathway runs between these two kinds of disappearance. The systematic violence against *los desaparecidos* did not appear out of nowhere overnight. The path was laid by intensifying political polarization between Argentina's version of Left versus Right in preceding years, a trend that severed relationships of all kinds. Scholars have studied how societies like Argentina's end up descending into violence and have pointed out this consistent pattern: widening relational separation between groups intensifies political conflict, which in turn increases broader societal vulnerability to political violence.[2] For example, one statistical study showed that democracies where people feel high levels of politically motivated animosity are 34 percent more likely to suffer political violence.[3] The connection between relational division and political violence makes intuitive sense when you ponder the basic question "How do you get to the point

2. Steven Levitsky and Daniel Ziblatt, *How Democracies Die* (New York: Broadway Books, 2018); Anne Applebaum, *Twilight of Democracy: The Seductive Lure of Authoritarianism* (New York: Anchor, 2021).
3. James A. Piazza, "Political Polarization and Political Violence" (June 1, 2022). *Security Studies* (2023). Forthcoming. Available at SSRN: https://ssrn.com/abstract =4156980 or http://dx.doi.org/10.2139/ssrn.4156980.

where one group of citizens can contemplate physically harming another group of citizens?" This happens only if those two groups are socially separated into an *us* and a *them*. Once *them* no longer appear in the social lives of *us*, it becomes easier to dehumanize them. Add in the fear, often stoked by political leaders, that "they are out to get us," and the situation grows more volatile. The collective desire to eliminate *them* intensifies, and so does the temptation to resort to violence to complete the disappearing act.

We are not claiming that America is on the imminent verge of descending into systemic political violence. The route running from widespread relational separation to increased political violence can take decades to traverse. But momentum builds with every passing year. There are many signs that in our country the gap is closing between the two kinds of disappearance, as the impact of severed relationships increases willingness to sever lives altogether. As the Big Sort deepens here in the United States, surveys of American political attitudes show a marked rise in openness to political violence. Public support for the use of force against members of Congress nearly doubled from January to June of 2023, according to a study published by the University of Chicago's Project on Security and Threats.[4] As of June 26, 2023, an estimated 44 million people supported using violence to coerce lawmakers. Democrats had the largest

4. Julia Shapero, "Five Percent of Americans Say Force Justified to Put Trump Back in Office: Poll," *The Hill*, September 28, 2022, www.thehill.com/blogs /blog-briefing-room/3664721-5-percent-of-americans-say-force-justified-to -put-trump-back-in-office-poll/.

increase: in January, 7 percent of Democrats supported using political violence against lawmakers; by June, this had climbed to 16 percent. Eighteen percent of all Republican respondents endorse the use of force against lawmakers.[5] In 2021, 81 percent of local officials reported being on the receiving end of harassment, threats, or violence.[6] Some 20 percent of Democrats (approximately 12.6 million voters) and 16 percent of Republicans (approximately 7.9 million voters) believe America would be better off if large numbers of their opposition died.[7] More than 42 percent of Americans view people in the opposing political party as "downright evil."[8]

These are historically high numbers that should alarm us all. It is quite likely that these numbers will be even higher during the next election season, as Americans continue to add to their list of the disappeared ones.

The comparison between our current state in America and Argentina's in the 1970s should fill us with both hope and humility. There is hope: currently, we have not descended into wholesale violence, and our political institutions and practices,

5. Shapero, "Force Justified."
6. "New Report: Harassment, Threats and Violence Directed at Local Elected Officials Rising at an Alarming Rate," National League of Cities, November 10, 2021, www.nlc.org/post/2021/11/10/new-report-harassment-threats-and-violence -directed-at-local-elected-officials-rising-at-an-alarming-rate/.
7. Nathan P. Kalmoe and Lilliana Mason, "Lethal Mass Partisanship: Prevalence, Correlates, & Electoral Contingencies," Danny Hayes (website), accessed December 12, 2023, www.dannyhayes.org/uploads/6/9/8/5/69858539/kalmoe___mason _ncapsa_2019_-_lethal_partisanship_-_final_lmedit.pdf.
8. Kalmoe and Mason, "Lethal Mass Partisanship."

such as our history of the peaceful transfer of political power, are stronger than they were in Argentina. But we also need humility. The events of January 6, 2021, revealed how even that bulwark is threatened. As a country, we now have a very recent experience of a violent insurrection, stirred by an outgoing president who consciously mobilized the us-versus-them mentality to resist the peaceful transfer of power. The violence of events like the January 6 insurrection should warn us that we are not exempt from what has befallen many other countries. We are stumbling—and in some cases running—farther down the path to violent conflict. We need to recognize that there is a point when it becomes too late to turn around.

We are voluntarily creating a class of vilified Americans—the disappeared ones—whom we otherwise loved, whom we otherwise respected. Either we are shunning them or we are vanishing purposefully and permanently from their lives. They are disappearing. We have disappeared. And our loved ones are left wondering if they'll ever see us again. Individually, we need to make a change to reverse the relational losses in our own lives. Collectively, we need to make a change to prevent a broader catastrophic loss of our democracy.

We need to reclaim hope rather than resign ourselves to the current state of affairs. Why? Because *we* are doing this to each other. There is no secret police out there doing this to us. We have the power to choose a different path. We can stop the disappearance.

We also need to adopt humility. Why? Because *we* are doing this to each other. The change must start with each one of us, especially for those of us who follow Jesus. With some faithful effort, we can move toward a better Christian politics.

THE FIRST STEPS

Humility can feed our hope. If we are willing to listen humbly for echoes between our situation and the history of other countries, we can also pick up notes of hope. The story of *los desaparecidos* hints at the first steps we can take. On April 30, 1977, thirteen mothers of disappeared individuals linked arms and walked into the Plaza de Mayo in the capital city of Buenos Aires. They bore on placards the names and photographs of their children. They were determined not to simply let their identities fade from view. Every subsequent Thursday, these mothers joined together, with more and more grieving mothers of *los desaparecidos* gathering. As the mothers walked through the plaza, they chanted the names of the missing. They grieved the losses. These weekly marches swelled to thousands. They became a political force known as the Mothers of the Plaza and gained international prominence. Sting wrote a song about them called "They Dance Alone (*Cueca Solo*)," and U2 honored these grieving women in a *Joshua Tree* song called "Mothers of the Disappeared." What is remarkable about their story—and the relevant analogy for us today—is how this transformation began with the modest steps of naming, remembering, and grieving. Their steps provide a clue for how we can begin to address our disappearance.

REFLECTION EXERCISE

You can take these same steps right now: naming, remembering, and grieving.

1. Naming: Look back over your list and slowly read each name out loud. As you do, invite the Holy Spirit to guide your feelings. Try to discern whether a particular name tugs at you.

2. Remembering: With that one name, ask the Holy Spirit to help you call that person to mind. What does he or she look like? How did you meet this person? What is your favorite memory of this person? What traits did you especially appreciate? And, yes, try to remember the painful events that led up to this person's disappearance from your life.

3. Grieving: If you feel able and willing, ask the Holy Spirit to help you locate your grief associated with this person. Grief is the recognition of the loss combined with the longing for that person. Pay special attention to that sense of longing.

As you go through these steps, resist the pressure to do something active right away. Experience these feelings. Sit with them. You may want to go through these steps over the course of multiple days. Give the time needed for each of these steps of naming, remembering, and grieving, because they build up to the next big step: hope.

You don't need to rush to hope right now. The Holy Spirit will help you experience hope when it is appropriate for you. But the question to ponder now is this: amid political conflict and relational carnage, what exactly are we supposed to hope for?

The Mothers of the Plaza give us another hint. When they took their first steps, some of them undoubtedly held on to the hope that they could still be reunited to their disappeared ones. They needed that initial hope to get started, and you may need it as well. Compared to the Mothers of the Plaza, you of course have so much more reason to hope for a reunion, because these conflicts haven't gotten horribly violent yet. Many of the people on your list of disappeared ones are probably still alive. You still have time.

But the amount of time for a reunion in our lifetime is not infinite. Around the time of their Costa Rica vacation, Emily discovered that several of her close friends had received life-threatening medical diagnoses. She started to imagine what it would feel like if she got the news that Jack and Cindy were ill.

Emily's close friend then shared with her how a broken family relationship was finally restored after eighteen years. The example gave her hope that God really could restore broken relationships. "But I also realized that Jack and Cindy could very well be dead if we waited eighteen years—a point of no return."

Unbeknownst to Sean and Emily, their eldest daughter was praying with her college friends for a reconciliation between her grandparents and parents. Meanwhile, Sean had felt God leading him through his own version of naming, remembering, and grieving. These steps were stirring hope in him. Sean and Emily then sought counsel and prayer from their church small group and finally decided to make another trip to Oregon to try to reconcile with Jack and Cindy. In preparation for the visit, Sean and Emily made a long list of the issues to address. Sean tucked the piece of paper, bulleted and categorized, inside a tote bag.

When Jack and Cindy opened the door, they moved toward Sean and Emily and embraced them with a warmth that surprised Emily. As she returned the hug, she could feel the physical frailty in her aging in-laws: there really were only so many years they had left together. She felt a surge of compassion and love for them. "It was like a spell had hidden all this love," Emily recounts, "and in our embrace, that spell suddenly got broken."

Later that weekend, the four of them talked about what

each had felt in the past few years. Jack and Cindy listened closely with tears welling up in their eyes. "I did not realize all of that was happening for you," Cindy lamented. "I just thought you didn't want us around." Each side could verbalize to the other what everyone most needed to hear: their relationships with each other mattered far more than the substance of their political differences.

During the weekend, their conversation never really dived into the specifics of the issues—the specific *what* that had divided them. None of the Harrises changed their political beliefs, none stopped caring about politics, and none disavowed their political allegiances. But *how* they moved toward each other was enough. For Sean and Emily, how Jack and Cindy had embraced them was enough; for Jack and Cindy, how Sean and Emily had made the effort to see them was enough. Sean never took out the list from his tote bag.

The Harris story is a hopeful one indeed. And we have more such stories to share. But we also need to be honest with you. We cannot guarantee the story of your estranged relationship will end with a Harris-style reunion, even if you hope for it and take further steps to pursue such an outcome. Tragically, politics *can* kill off relationships for a lifetime.

The Mothers of the Plaza discovered this tragic truth. As the years went on, it became apparent to most of the women that a happy reunion was highly unlikely. Most of them would not even get the bodies of their loved ones returned to them.

INTRODUCTION

Yet the Mothers of the Plaza still took their steps together every Thursday. They could do so only because as they walked, they had begun to lift their hope to something higher. They longed for some future—which maybe they could not even precisely articulate—that incorporated their very real pain into a greater meaning. They longed for redemption.

Redemption is when pain does not necessarily disappear but it does lead to transformation. For the mothers, in their hope for redemption, they themselves were transformed. They started out as uncertain, confused, and isolated women; they ended up as a powerful political movement. Their country was also transformed. The Mothers of the Plaza ultimately helped to end the nation's political violence and also restored to many thousands of families the truth (and even, in a few cases, the bodily remains) of those who had disappeared. Argentina today has its share of struggles (political polarization hasn't disappeared), but it is a much, much better place than it was when the mothers first started their walk.

Christian hope is the hope for redemption. Though we cannot guarantee that all your broken relationships will be made whole in your lifetime, we can promise that if you seek God in the process, you will be transformed. As you follow Jesus and submit your politics to him, you will be changed into the very image of our Lord (2 Cor. 3:18). God intends this transformation for every disciple of Jesus. And so we can confidently ask God to grow our hope for our own transformation.

23

This kind of hope is "an anchor for the soul" that, amid the conflicting currents of Right and Left, keeps us truly centered on Jesus (Heb. 6:19).

As people in the process of being transformed by God, we can genuinely offer hope to others. We can model a way out of the finger-pointing and fist shaking that dominates our political culture. Instead of insisting that the other side must change, we can humbly demonstrate how God changes us and look for ways to be reconciled. Wouldn't that be a hopeful, redemptive message to the world?

HOW TO USE THIS BOOK

This book is meant as a companion volume to *The After Party* video course. We encourage readers to engage with the course (see the information at the end of the book) and read this book before, during, or after doing the video version because the two are meant to complement each other. The video course, in particular, is designed to be experienced with other people—in small groups at church, in Sunday school, with a group in your neighborhood, or even with just one other person. And the book and video course can be engaged with simultaneously or in any sequence: you can read the book first to ascertain whether your group is ready for the course, or your group can do the course first and then together read the book to go deeper. It's important, however, to tackle this material with others to combat one of the biggest underlying problems: our isolation and division from one another.

This message will be most useful to those seeking relationships with one another. Indeed, we need the support of friends and companions, which is a common theme in the stories of hope we share in this book: the Mothers of the Plaza linking arms, Emily and Sean seeking counsel from their small group, and other stories you'll read in the following pages.

At the same time, we also recognize that some Christians are not currently involved in a small group community. A good number of Christians in recent years have left church altogether, often because of political tensions. We've written this book for you as well, to help you consider a path back to Christian community, whether that is a reunion with old friends or finding new ones. We are not meant to walk alone.

The After Party itself is the product of a particular set of deep friendships. At the core is Curtis Chang, David French, and Russell Moore. We've also included voices from our network of friendships that encompass even more diversity along racial, gender, theological, and political lines. We recognize we do not represent the full diversity of American Christianity and that we do not have all the answers (or even most of them!). The church will surely need many other messages and messengers to address the complexity of our current challenges.

We are certain that every reader will finish this book with the thought "But you didn't cover X!" This book does not presume to have arrived at the answers that comprehensively define Christian politics. We are about movement, not arrival. As our subtitle indicates, our goal is to help us get moving *toward* something better. We ourselves are journeying as a group of friends—and we are glad that you have decided to join us.

We need better Christian politics. "Better" doesn't mean we need to change our political views. But it does mean we need to change our hearts. "Better" doesn't mean we should stop caring about political issues. But it does mean we need to care more about the people who have disappeared. It's not too late. It's not hopeless. The time to start is now.

CHAPTER 1

INVITED TO THE PARTY

WHO'S IN AND WHO'S OUT

Have you ever scrolled through social media only to see photos of your friends hanging out without you? That feeling of exclusion is one of the more painful human experiences, because our nervous system is extremely sensitive to signals around belonging. Some anthropologists theorize that this stems from when our ancestors lived as hunter-gatherers in small tribes. If one person killed an animal to eat, he might have needed another to keep watch as he prepared it so others wouldn't take it. At night, people also needed to ensure a place around the campfire—a place of safety, provision, and protection from the predators prowling in the darkness. Being accepted into the group meant you didn't have to fend for yourself in a harsh landscape.

Whether this theory is correct doesn't really matter; the point is that these instincts exist in us now. We all experience them. Powerfully. We feel hurt when our friends gather without us, because we're wired to desire inclusion and fear exclusion.

Because we need to feel safe around the others by our campfire, we also are sensitive to betrayals. We need solidarity: the feeling that everyone around us is on one side, our side. Our brains are hardwired to feel alarm when we discover someone close to us may hold opposing views. Who's in? Who's out? It's natural to seek answers to these fundamental questions, and to do so on the basis of similarity and solidarity. Who is in? Those who share similarities with you. Who is out? Those who violate solidarity with you.

Given this deeply embedded mindset, we tend to handle our invitation lists carefully. Who gets invited to our parties—both social and political—and whose parties we will attend are often defined by similarity and solidarity.

The problem today is that the invitation lists to our social parties are increasingly written with political markers, and the membership ranks of our respective political parties increasingly resemble our social segregation.

Is this true for you?

REFLECTION EXERCISE

1. Recall the last two social parties that you hosted or attended (a small dinner party, a Super Bowl watch party, a potluck at church, etc.). What percentage of the attendees belonged to a different political party from yours?

2. Create your ideal guest list of twelve people you most want to hang out with for an evening.
   Now circle the people on this list who belong to a different political party from yours.

3. Imagine a party where you know that the host and a large majority of attendees will belong to a different political party from yours. For whatever reason, you have received an invitation. As you consider whether to attend, take thirty seconds to write down your feelings and thoughts about showing up at this event.

THE STORIES WE TELL OURSELVES

Why did you choose your political "in" group? Why have you rejected your political "out" group?

The question about underlying political motivations is a bit complicated because the answer depends on who is telling the story. If you ask the sociologists, they will tell you that we choose our politics because of our deep—and often unconscious—need for similarity and solidarity. Things feel so much better and easier when we can align our politics with those of the people around us—when we can present a solidly united front. The similarity is reinforced by the Big Sort, as we gather around more and more homogenous campfires. The solidarity is driven by a related sociological phenomenon called the "law of in-group polarization."[1] Findings have shown that, in a group consisting solely of people who share the same political beliefs, many members tend to adopt more extreme versions of those beliefs and ostracize anyone betraying group solidarity. These dynamics are well proven and happen on both the Left and the Right.

But there's another interesting dynamic at play as well. When we explain our personal political choices, we tend to exempt ourselves from these larger demographic and psychological forces. We don't like a story that casts us as sheep herded into similar-looking flocks by the Big Sort, collectively bleating to the "law of in-group polarization." That's what happens to *them*, we say. Surely it doesn't happen to *me*.

As Western individualists who value forging our own

---

1. Cass R. Sunstein, "The Law of Group Polarization," Chicago Unbound, 1999, https://chicagounbound.uchicago.edu/law_and_economics/542.

destinies, we prefer to depict ourselves as individuals making rational decisions. We gravitate to the narrative that our politics are motivated by the *what*: what ideology, party, and policies we support. We like to think we have sorted through all the options and have chosen the best positions on issues like tax rates, foreign policy, and education. If we are Christians, we additionally want to believe that our ideas are derived from our faith in Jesus.

The standard Christian version of this preferred narrative could be represented in the following picture:

OUR STORY OF POLITICS

THE WHAT OF POLITICS → IDEOLOGY PARTY POLICY ← JESUS

We like to think that Jesus' teachings inform our ideology: our big ideas of how things ought to be. These days, we might label the rival ideologies conservative versus liberal or Right versus Left. In this self-narrative, our intellectual commitment to these big ideas in turn leads us to choose a party as the group that most accurately reflects that ideology. In our American two-party system, this is the choice between the Republican and Democratic Parties. From there, we entrust our party to advance the correct policy: the specific way everyone should be governed. Prominent examples would be the policies governing abortion or immigration.

This *what* of politics framework is how most people explain (to themselves or to others) how they arrived at their political views. This is the kind of story told by people across the political spectrum today.

Our narrative framework of politics matters because it is the starting point for change. We cannot reverse the massive momentum of the Big Sort, either for the entire country or even for ourselves. We cannot overnight create social circles that are impervious to the law of in-group polarization. But all of us can begin to adopt a different story.

If you want to move toward better Christian politics, you don't have to uproot your life or make radical changes in your social circle. The starting point of change resides in your own mind, with the story you are telling yourself about politics. You can change your politics by changing your story.

THE WHAT OF POLITICS IN JESUS' DAY

To understand this invitation, it is helpful first to grasp the *what* of politics story that dominated politics in Jesus' day. Contemporary American politics may be polarized compared to our recent history, but it's tame compared to politics in first-century Israel. Jesus lived in a society suffering under Roman occupation, which split people along ideological, party, and policy lines. Jews of the first century had different ideas about what to do with the Roman Empire. Some wanted to cooperate with the invaders, while others wanted to oppose them.

This ideological split was expressed in two sets of opposing religio-political parties:[2]

COOPERATE WITH THE ROMANS	PHARISEES
SADDUCEES	SICCARI
HERODIANS	ZEALOTS
TAX COLLECTORS	OPPOSE THE ROMANS

You might be surprised to see the Pharisees categorized as a political party, since the Pharisees have been popularly mis-characterized as a group that cared only about religious legalism in private morality and spirituality. But the Pharisees' strict adherence to the law was because of their belief that God would eject the Roman oppressors (and the Jews who had cooperated with them) only when enough Jews returned to God's side. Strict obedience to the Jewish law was how they drew the circle around "God's side." The Pharisees conceived of themselves as true Jewish patriots, intent on restoring Israel to its former glory as an independent nation.

Note the last oppositional pairing of parties in the box: the tax collectors versus the Zealots. These two sides squared off on the hot-button policy issue of their day: Roman taxation. Like most colonial powers, Rome wanted to reap financial benefits

---

2. We are using the term *parties* here in the broader sociological sense of movements organized around aims, which in the ancient mindset would have included religious agendas.

from their occupation, and like many colonizers, they used natives to do the dirty work of collection. The Roman government had created a class of Jewish "tax collectors" to execute their tax policies.

Zealots were bitterly resentful of this Roman tax policy—and those who collaborated with it. Many Zealots believed violent action was warranted against the Romans and their Jewish collaborators. According to ancient historians, the Zealot movement was founded in Jesus' neighborhood when he was a boy. This happened around 6 CE when Judas of Galilee (not Judas Iscariot, who later betrayed Jesus) led a tax revolt during which he and his followers burned the homes of tax collectors and plundered their property.

As the Zealots targeted the tax collectors, the Roman military (which was charged with protecting the tax collectors) targeted the Zealots. Roman legions crushed the first Zealot movement, and Judas of Galilee ended up crucified on a Roman cross. Crucifixion was a powerful political statement, one the Romans reserved for political rebels. Mere criminals were not crucified (the two individuals crucified next to Jesus were not petty thieves; a more accurate translation is that they were politically motivated bandits). The sheer brutality of the punishment—and why it was expressly reserved for political crimes—was Rome's warning: cooperate with their policies or die.

Judas of Galilee's revolt, and the cycle of violence it unleashed, took place just decades before the Gospels were

written. Everyone, on all sides, would have remembered it. The
tax collector who encountered the adult Jesus may very well have
inherited the vocation from his father. He might have grown up
scarred by a family history of having their property plundered
by Zealots in the name of patriotism. The Zealot movement
rebounded from its initial defeat and was growing in Jesus' time,
especially in Galilee. Around the dinner table of Zealot families, men undoubtedly told the tales of their fallen heroes and
complained about the latest oppressive taxes and rules.

In all eras, the political stories we tell ourselves shape us,
even across generations. In societies that are already divided
by larger forces, this framework tends to accelerate adherents
down a path of ever-increasing polarization, especially when
there is no other kind of story to counterbalance its tendencies
toward cycles of resentment, conflict, and even violence. The
warning for our modern American context comes to us not
only from first-century Israel; we can hear the alarm emanat-
ing from other societies in today's world.

DAVID'S STORY

Before 2007, if I were to sum up the nature of my engagement with politics, I would have started and fin-
ished by discussing policy. When I thought of Christian
engagement in politics, I thought only about "the ends."
I didn't think so much about "the means." I didn't believe

the ends justified the means. Rather, I wrongly presumed that Christians would pursue virtuous ends through virtuous means. The most important aspect of politics, in my mind, remained the policy issues themselves.

But in 2007 when I got to Iraq, I very quickly realized "the means" often overwhelmed "the ends." One might have thought, for example, that the civil war between the Sunni and Shia Muslims was driven by profound theological or public-policy differences— such as the division of oil revenues, the power-sharing relationships between the different factions, and the composition of the police or the military. But when I talked to Sunni fighters or members of Shia militias, I consistently heard deep grievances over the wrongs committed in the pursuit of these different policies. It was the cruelty and the violence of their political opponents that motivated cruelty and violence in return.

When I came home to the United States, it was like the scales had fallen from my eyes. While we thankfully were not grappling with the kind of outright combat we saw in Iraq, the deep grievances between Left and Right were and are readily apparent. If you talk to Democrats about their problems with the Republicans, it is far more likely that you will hear anger about, say, challenges to Barack Obama's citizenship, conspiracy theories about the election, or the political violence of January 6. All of those misdeeds create a sense that "they" are just simply bad people.

Similarly, if you talk to Republicans about their problems with Democrats, they might respond with their own stories of grievance and persecution. They might mention the attempted mass shooting of Republican congressmen by a Bernie Sanders supporter,[3] Democratic excesses in their investigations of Donald Trump,[4] or the riots that ripped through American cities in 2020.[5]

The emotional grievances we feel over these very real incidents are a far more powerful factor in our political choices and loyalties than the intellectual disagreements that arise when we debate tax cuts, trade policy, or foreign affairs. And, more importantly, the debates over these issues work to reaffirm the belief that the other side is morally depraved.

Us against them? Yes. Because "they" are horrible, horrible people.

---

3. Jose Pagliery, "Suspect in Congressional Shooting Was Bernie Sanders Supporter, Strongly Anti-Trump," CNN, June 15, 2017, www.cnn.com/2017/06/14/homepage2/james-hodgkinson-profile.

4. Charlie Savage, "We Just Got a Rare Look at National Security Surveillance. It Was Ugly," *New York Times*, December 11, 2019, www.nytimes.com/2019/12/11/us/politics/fisa-surveillance-fbi.html; Charlie Savage, "After Years of Political Hype, the Durham Inquiry Failed to Deliver," *New York Times*, May 17, 2023, www.nytimes.com/2023/05/17/us/politics/durham-report-trump-russia.html.

5. Stephanie Pagones, "Protests, Riots That Gripped America in 2020," Fox News, December 29, 2020, www.foxnews.com/us/protests-riots-nationwide-america-2020.

David's experience in Iraq illustrates another dynamic that recurs in politically divided societies across time and space: the danger that emerges when the *what* of politics framework becomes fused indistinguishably with religious identity.

It's one thing to believe that our religious commitments can and should inform our political commitments—there's nothing inherently wrong or dangerous about that. But it's another thing—a wrong and dangerous thing—to claim that our religion and our politics are one and the same. Look back at the diagram of the *what* of politics framework. The arrow between Jesus and political ideology, party, and policy does and should exist. But an arrow is not an equal sign.

In war-torn Iraq, David witnessed what happens when that arrow mutates into an equal sign. The biblical version of this mutation is illustrated by the derogatory term often used by Pharisees to demarcate who was "out": "tax collectors and sinners" (Matt. 9:11; Luke 5:30). Note how a religious identity ("sinners") is fused together with a political designation ("tax collector"). For the Pharisees and the Zealots, the tax collector was simultaneously a political opponent and a religious heretic.

When political markers become fused with religious markers, all other lines get drawn accordingly. This is why Pharisees forbade social associations with sinners and tax collectors. One was not supposed to attend the same parties or share the same meals with political opponents and the religiously "unclean." The fusion of politics and religion determined who was in and who was out.

THE PARTY LIFE OF JESUS

Our politics today echo the dynamics of the politics in Jesus' day. Two camps have squared off, with both sides drawing the boundaries by using religious and political markers, which in turn redraws our social boundaries. The resulting lines solidify into walls dividing who is in and who is out, who is *us* and who is *them*.

These boundaries get so hardened in our own minds that when someone comes along and messes with those lines, it can feel uncomfortable. That person can mess with the stories we tell in our minds.

Jesus was such a person in his day. He still is today.

Jesus loved parties, the social kind. We know this because his teachings consistently featured illustrations drawn from the party context. The Gospels are full of accounts of him attending dinner parties, helping wedding parties by getting everyone replenished with the best drinks, and hosting his own intimate meals. He received so many party invitations, and accepted so many, that his critics accused him of being "a glutton and a drunkard" (Matt. 11:19). He seems to have possessed the personality that made people want to invite him to their parties and also want to attend his parties.

But his party life messed with party lines. He accepted party invitations from Pharisees (Luke 7:36; 14:1–14). But he also invited himself to the house of Zacchaeus, a chief tax collector (Luke 19:1–6), an act that raised eyebrows: "All the people saw this and began to mutter, 'He has gone to be the guest of a sinner'" (Luke 19:7). In multiple accounts, the Pharisees criticized him in front of his disciples: "Why does he eat with tax collectors and sinners?" (Mark 2:16).

This was no accident. Jesus threw social parties that deliberately messed with political party lines. Jesus hung out with the twelve disciples most of all. They worked, traveled, ate around campfires, and socialized together (John 21:9).

Who were the members of this inner circle? Read how the gospel of Matthew describes the core "Jesus Party": "The names of the twelve apostles are these: first, Simon, who is called Peter, and Andrew his brother; James the son of Zebedee, and John his brother; Philip and Bartholomew; Thomas and *Matthew the tax collector*; James the son of Alphaeus, and Thaddaeus; *Simon the Zealot*, and Judas Iscariot, who betrayed him" (Matt. 10:1–4 ESV, emphasis added).

Most of the disciples are identified in traditional fashion, by their family identity ("son of so-and-so"). But the Bible goes out of its way to identify two by their politics: "Matthew the tax collector and Simon the Zealot."

What did it feel like for Simon and Matthew to be invited to this Jesus party?

REFLECTION EXERCISE

Take a minute to imagine the first dinner party that Jesus threw with all twelve included.

Here are some prompts:

- Where do you picture Matthew and Simon sitting?
- How are they looking at each other?
- What is going through each of their minds?
- In your imagined scenario, where is Jesus sitting?
- What does Jesus' facial expression look like?
- What do you think is going on in Jesus' mind?

As we proceed, we will discover more about what was going on in Jesus' mind. Jesus had important reasons for inviting both a tax collector and a Zealot into his inner circle, reasons that would not be revealed until his death on the cross, his resurrection, the creation of the early church, and the ensuing centuries of Christian mission. Even to this day, we still don't fully grasp his revolutionary agenda. He's still at work to fully open our minds.

So let's imagine that first Jesus party. None of the disciples really grasped Jesus' agenda. Yet here they were. In my version of this imaginative exercise, Matthew and Simon anchor opposite ends of the dinner table, with their arms folded; their eyes alternate between avoiding each other and glaring at each other, their bodies tense with suspicion and alarm. And sitting in the middle is Jesus, wearing (in my imagination) a knowing smile.

How did Jesus pull this off? He seemingly possessed the force of personality that could draw people to gather around him. But such personality-based influences can go only so far.

Think of those extended families that are racked by simmering conflicts, whether because of politics or other disputes, but still somehow manage to gather on Thanksgiving Day because some loving and respected grandmother keeps the peace and no one wants to disappoint her. But what happens when she's gone? Jesus knew he would be gone one day. He knew he wouldn't always be sitting there in the middle of the table to keep peace. And in his absence, either during his earthly ministry or after his crucifixion, a passing comment might easily break up the party. Maybe Matthew would hear about the most recent act of Zealot violence against a fellow tax collector, and he might mutter, just loud enough for Simon to hear, "It's time some Roman swords put a stop to these thugs." Or imagine Simon, upon hearing the announcement that tax rates had been raised again, smirking at Matthew and asking, "So, what do you sellouts think about that, huh?" Angry words might be flung across the dinner table, with the two disciples sullenly stalking out of the room, headed in opposite directions. Simon and Matthew would then disappear from each other's lives, perhaps for good.

This didn't happen. Except for Judas Iscariot, the traitor, the Jesus party hung together. Even after Jesus was killed—in a process that frustrated both political camps when Jesus refused to take up the sword and instead died via a method reserved for political rebels under a banner that declared him a rival king—the disciples remained loyal to Jesus and to one another. After Jesus ascended, Simon and Matthew founded a movement that ended up transforming Roman religion, culture, social institutions, politics, and even the world.

Years of sitting under the teaching of Jesus transformed the mindsets of Matthew the tax collector and Simon the Zealot. Note that this transformation was much more than the superficial "avoid politics at the dinner table" tactic that, at best, works only to help you white-knuckle your way through a Thanksgiving dinner. Jesus did not require Simon and Matthew to check their politics at the door. The invite list in Matthew 10 identifies them by their political labels as "Simon the Zealot" and "Matthew the tax collector" and expects later readers to still recognize them by their political labels and differences.

A change deeper and more durable than short-term conflict management happened to the disciples. Jesus transformed their political thinking into something new. What was the exact nature of this peculiar shift?

THE BIG SHIFT

We are all pulled into our separate parties by larger forces like the Big Sort. We need a correspondingly dramatic change in our story. Let's give a name to this narrative change: the Big Shift, which can be depicted visually like this:

OUR STORY OF POLITICS

THE WHAT OF POLITICS
IDEOLOGY
PARTY
POLICY

JESUS →

THE HOW OF POLITICS
SPIRITUAL VALUES
RELATIONSHIP
PRACTICES

Jesus shifted his disciples away from remaining exclusively preoccupied with the existing *what* of politics to an increasing commitment to his distinctive *how* of politics. This *how* of politics begins with the spiritual values that Jesus taught, including love, forgiveness, mercy, justice, truth, and two more values *The After Party* will especially focus on: hope and humility.

An emphasis on spiritual values messes with the emphasis on ideology. Most political ideologies are defined by opposing contrasts: for example, a liberal favors a more active government while a conservative insists on a more limited government. The ideology emphasis casts people into mutually exclusive camps. To remain a Zealot, you can only oppose your enemy. To remain a tax collector, you can only cooperate with your enemy. But notice what happens when you make the Big Shift to the spiritual value of love. With this change, both the Zealot and the tax collector can adopt the same spiritual value: "love your enemies" (which Jesus commands his disciples to do in Matthew 5:43–44). They both can shift to a spiritual plane—a move that does not require them to completely abandon their differing *what* ideological commitments. But here's the key: both must adopt the same Jesus *how*, such that *how* they oppose or cooperate with Rome now must be informed by love. Love encompasses both ideological options: it is quite possible to simultaneously oppose and cooperate with someone you love. Just ask any happily married couple.

The example of love demonstrates how the Big Shift emphasizes relationships. The spiritual values of Jesus almost always flow into relationships. How do you forgive your enemy unless you are engaging with your enemy enough to feel hurt by him (Mark 11:25)? How do you practice humility except in a context where you are in conversation with the other side and you consider yourself to be right and they are wrong?

This shift to relationships messes with the *what* of party. A political party is defined by the collective drive to win, to defeat the opposing political party. A relationship is defined by the personal drive to connect with another person. In the party framework, people are divided into mutually exclusive categories: one cannot simultaneously be registered as a Republican and a Democrat. In a relationship, both are invited to join together. A Republican can relate with a Democrat without abandoning her party affiliation, and vice versa.

The Big Shift to relationships naturally translates into new practices. Our instincts for similarity and solidarity don't lead us to forgive our enemies; a disciple therefore needs to learn how to do so. Learning requires rehearsal. This is why Jesus so overwhelmingly emphasized new practices instead of endorsing existing policies. The Sermon on the Mount (Matthew 5–7) summarizes Jesus' most often repeated teachings. In those chapters, Jesus does not advocate for either rival political camp's specific policies. And if you try to draw a clear and incontestable arrow from Jesus' teaching to a specific policy debate between today's Right and Left, you can do so only by greatly distorting Jesus' words to fit your political agenda. But while he refrains from commentary on policies, he teaches very specifically on relational practices. Note again how the Big Shift opens up things in such a way that all are invited. Instead of supporting the policies of one side or the other, Jesus offers a list of practices that can be performed by everyone.

This emphasis on practices will disrupt how we currently

engage in policy conflicts. Here is just a sampling of the practices commanded by Jesus in the Sermon on the Mount:

- Show mercy (Matthew 5:7).
- Make peace (5:9).
- Refrain from angrily mocking your opponent (5:21–22).
- Prioritize reconciling over winning disputes (5:23–25).
- Avoid sexual scandals (5:27–30).
- Tell the truth (5:33–37).

Stop for a moment and ask yourself, *Does my experience of Christian political behavior today reflect these practices?* Imagine if all Christians committed themselves to adopting just one of these practices—say, the Matthew 5:21–22 practice of refraining from angrily mocking your opponent—while still promoting their preferred policies. Imagine if all progressive Christians advocating for police reform refrained from smearing all police officers as fascists and racists. Imagine if all conservative Christians advocating for immigration reform refrained from stereotyping immigrants as rapists and drug dealers. The resulting transformation of our political culture would be profound.

THE FALSE EXEMPTION

Sadly, American evangelical political culture somehow exempts followers and leaders from these practices. We vote for candidates who blatantly and gleefully violate these practices commanded by Jesus because we believe practices based on spiritual values (versus political expediency) are not adequate for the moment.

Russell Moore has seen this up close. Multiple pastors have told him that when they quote the Sermon on the Mount, specifically the part that says to turn the other cheek, they get pushback from their congregants. Invariably, someone will come up after the service and ask, "Where did you get those liberal talking points?"

In most of these scenarios, the pastor will respond, "I'm actually quoting Jesus Christ."

Moore explains why this is so unnerving. "What's alarming to me is that the response is not 'Oh, I need to listen to Jesus.' Instead, the response from congregants is often 'Yes, but that doesn't work anymore. That's weak. That doesn't apply to politics. That doesn't work when the stakes are so high.'"

But Jesus explicitly intended his teaching to apply to the realm of politics. The "liberal talking point" of "turn the other cheek" comes from Matthew 5:38–39, at the heart of his Sermon on the Mount. In the very next verses, Jesus references a Roman political policy whereby any Roman soldier could make a Jew carry a load for exactly a mile but was strictly forbidden to require this for any longer distance. If Jesus meant for his practices to apply under brutal foreign occupation, how could any of us today plausibly argue that our current political stakes are so high that we deserve an exemption?

In response to this oppressive Roman policy, Jesus calls for a shift to a new practice. The particular practice taught by Jesus is "go with them two miles" (Matt. 5:41). It is a clever and creative response typical of Jesus, who is clearly not subscribing to the Zealot policy of opposing the enemy with daggers. But is it cooperating with the enemy if this practice forces the Roman soldier to violate his own policy, and in a public way that further showcases the oppressive nature of this policy? Biblical scholar N. T. Wright describes what Jesus is doing with this practice: "Turn the tables on them [your Roman oppressors], advises Jesus. Don't fret and fume and plot revenge. Copy your generous God! Go a second mile, and astonish the soldier (and perhaps alarm him—what if his commanding officer found out?) with the news that there is a different way to be human, a way which doesn't plot revenge, which doesn't join the armed resistance movement . . . but which wins God's kind of victory over violence and injustice."[6]

In the Sermon on the Mount, Jesus shows how the Big Shift from policy to practice opens up creative new possibilities that minds narrowly locked in the *what* framework could never dream of.

Jesus intended his teaching to apply to political behavior. To drive this point home, he follows up his subversive teaching

6. N. T. Wright, *Matthew for Everyone: Part 1, Chapters 1–15* (London: Society for Promoting Christian Knowledge; Louisville, KY: Westminster John Knox Press, 2004), 52.

on going the extra mile by referencing the political parties that were hated by his mostly pro-Zealot audience: "If you love those who love you, what reward will you get? *Are not even the tax collectors doing that?* And if you greet only your own people, what are you doing more than others? Do not even *pagans* do that?" (Matt. 5:46–47, emphases mine).

In the audience's political story, it was clear who was cast in the role of enemies: the tax collectors and the pagans (the latter was another term for the Romans).

His command radically changes their narrative: "You have heard that it was said, 'Love your neighbor and hate your enemy.' But I tell you, love your enemies and pray for those who persecute you, that you may be children of your Father in heaven" (Matt. 5:43–45). Jesus is calling them to shift to the *how* of spiritual values (love), to relationship (with their political enemies), and to new practices (prayer for those enemies).

The rest of this book will explore other biblical examples of this Big Shift from the *what* to the *how*. But let us make one important caveat: the Big Shift is just that, a shift. It is shifting the relative weight we place on the *what* versus the *how*; it is not taking our feet entirely off the *what*. Christians can still care about the *what* of politics. All of us (David, Russell, and Curtis) have spent good parts of our professional lives advocating that Christians should support particular policies like religious liberty, racial justice, free speech, defense of weaker nations against foreign oppression, generous care for the poor, and vaccination to protect the common good. The three of us care about the *what*.

But as we pursue the *what* of politics, the Jesus *how* must take priority. No political stakes can justify exempting ourselves from the *how* of spiritual values, relationships, and practices commanded by Jesus.

Jesus himself embodies this emphasis on the *how*, in how he relates with each one of us. Jesus himself prioritizes the *how* over the *what* with us. Here's a question: How confident are you that you are in perfect similarity and solidarity with Jesus on the *what*s of Christian life? Consider the religious equivalent of ideology: say, the theology of the Trinity or the doctrine of the Eucharist. Consider the religious equivalent of policy: say, the correct approach to personal finances or sexual behavior. On these *what*s, how confident are you that you live in perfect similarity and solidarity with Jesus?

Wouldn't it be terrifying if Jesus were the kind of person who would disinvite us from his presence the moment he discovered we thought differently than he does on the *what*? The more self-aware we become as Christians, the more we will recognize that we are not only frequently misaligned with Jesus but also opposed to his agenda in some deep parts of our very being. Scripture diagnoses every human being in stark terms: "You were alienated from God and were enemies in your minds because of your evil behavior" (Col. 1:21).

This doesn't mean that the *what* doesn't matter or that we

shouldn't always seek more alignment. But shouldn't we be thankful that Jesus prioritizes the *how* with us? The spiritual values of forgiveness, grace, and mercy take priority in his relationship with us, and he continually practices these values toward us. Let's go back to the spiritual value of love. To paraphrase Paul's classic words about God's love in 1 Corinthians 13, if we get all *whats* in the world correct but have not the *how* of love, then we are nothing. Love overwhelmingly assumes the highest priority, such that, in Jesus, God loved us while we were his enemies (Rom. 5:10). If Jesus prioritizes the *how* in relating to us, we should mirror this priority in relating to others. "As I have loved you," Jesus says, "so you must love one another" (John 13:34). As Jesus emphasized in the Sermon on the Mount, he explicitly intends the "one another" to include our political enemies.

The *what* of politics is complicated to understand, and we (Curtis, David, and Russell) do not presume to have all the answers on ideology, parties, and policies. On those matters, different Christians will hold different views. On some issues, we differ among ourselves on the right answers to very complicated questions. In contrast, the *how* of Jesus' politics is not complicated to understand—it's just challenging to obey. And while the four of us also do not presume to have mastered the *how* of spiritual values, relationships, and practices in our political behavior, the direction of emphasis is unambiguous. To follow Jesus, we move toward the *how*.

Practices over policy. Relationships over party. Spiritual values over ideology. The *how* over the *what*. This is the Big Shift that happens in the Jesus party. It is what makes the Jesus party hang together across political differences. We can disagree on the *what* if we all are moving toward Jesus in the *how*.

REFLECTION EXERCISE

Think back to the reflection exercise in the introduction where you identified your disappeared one. Can you imagine you and that person as Simon the Zealot and Matthew the tax collector? Jesus invites you both to join his party, where you can once again share a meal together. Are you ready to come on in?

CHAPTER 2

THE DISCIPLE

RUSSELL'S STORY

In high school, I was very interested in politics.

I had my whole life planned out: I'd graduate from high school, college, and law school, then run for state representative in my home state of Mississippi. Eventually, I would be elected lieutenant governor, then governor, then president of the United States. I daydreamed about walking into a room to the tune of "Hail to the Chief."

In the 1988 presidential contest, which pitted Democrat Michael Dukakis against Republican George Herbert Walker Bush, commentators frequently talked about how, in almost every presidential election, the taller candidate wins. Since Bush (at six foot two) towered over Dukakis (at five foot eight), people speculated that Bush would win. This became an actual point of contention in the race, as the two candidates used different-sized podiums during debates and Dukakis even stood on a small riser.

"You're going to meet with the Soviets," people mocked Dukakis, "and roll out your little booster stool?"

At seventeen years old, this upset me. I remember thinking, *If I am ever a candidate for president of the United States, I'm never going to be running against an opponent who's shorter than I am. So that's really depressing.*

Then I realized I was worried about a race for president of the United States that included me. The least of the obstacles between me and the Oval Office was my height. After all of these years, I now realize my problem was not that I'm too short to be president. My problem was my inflated self-perception: I was too big in my own mind to humbly follow the King of Kings.

HOPE AND HUMILITY

The After Party project believes that hope and humility are crucial spiritual values for political discipleship under Jesus. Russell's childhood story evokes the interesting interplay between these two values. His sense of hope is wonderful: we should aspire to be people who believe they can make a positive contribution to the world. Russell's friends admire how this value that was present in him from early on has continued to animate his entire career at the intersection of faith and politics. But in his story, we also catch a glimpse of the need for that hope to be balanced with humility. His worries about his height revealed that his adolescent vision of making a positive contribution to the world was very specific: it insisted on featuring him at the very top of the world.

You may not have ever felt the extremes of hope and humility the way Russell did in high school, but we all are called to grow in these spiritual values. This spiritual growth anchors the Big Shift and moves it from an overemphasis on the *what* of politics to a Jesus-centered *how* of politics.

REFLECTION EXERCISE

To help you reflect and talk with others about where you are on this growth trajectory, we've created a Hope/Humility conversation starter tool. Please take this quiz before reading further since it will set up how you benefit from the rest of the book. The exercise asks you a few brief questions. It's quick to take, requiring only a couple of minutes.

The easiest way to use the Hope/Humility

conversation starter is at Redeeming Babel here: https://redeemingbabel.org/the-after-party/quiz/. (Or scan the following QR code.) If you prefer to take the survey in writing, go to the appendix of this book. (But the online tool really is more convenient!)

The Hope/Humility exercise depicts how these spiritual values define your politics. Keep in mind that this is just an informal snapshot: the exercise is not meant as a scientific diagnostic, and you are inevitably much more complex than your results. This is meant to catalyze self-reflection and conversations with others that lead to spiritual growth.

The exercise assigns one of four profiles to describe your state. Don't read about the profiles quite yet; for now, just record yours here: _____.

In the last chapter, we explored how Jesus transformed two disciples: Simon the Zealot and Matthew the tax collector. Now let's turn our attention to another pair of disciples: James and John. Jesus' playful nickname for them—"sons of thunder" (Mark 3:17)—tells us a great deal about their personalities. They seemed to be a loud and confident pair. Some scholars believe the nickname might allude to the Jewish word for "zeal," which suggests they might have belonged to the Zealot political party.

We can pick up other clues that tell us James and John at least leaned strongly toward the ideology of opposing Rome. For instance, in Luke 9:51–56, Jesus and his disciples enter a village of the Samaritans. James and John are part of the advance team. While the Samaritans were not exactly in the camp cooperating with Rome, they were descendants of people who had similarly collaborated with another foreign power that had invaded Israel centuries earlier. Combine that with a complicated racial animosity (they were not considered truly Jewish), and the Samaritans were viewed as a hated *them* by those who identified with the *us* of Jewish nationalism.

This political backdrop explains why this particular Samaritan village gave Jesus and his disciples a chilly welcome: "But the people did not receive him, because his face was set toward Jerusalem" (Luke 9:53 ESV). The residents (mistakenly) assumed that Jesus was marching forth on the capital to assume Jewish nationalist political power, and Samaritans were opposed to such a movement. The political leanings of James and John are revealed by how quickly the pair then went to Jesus with an eagerness to unleash violence on their political opponents: "Lord, do you want us to tell fire to come down from heaven and consume them?" (v. 54 ESV).

Jesus' response was clear: "But he turned and rebuked them" (v. 55 ESV). Jesus unambiguously warned James and John not to cross over the line into political violence. He would eventually go further and entirely upend their us-versus-them mindset.

Despite the redirections needed from time to time, Jesus seemed to welcome and appreciate James's and John's underlying energy. It's why he gave them their nickname in the first place. Jesus must have appreciated how decisively James and John had responded to his initial invitation: they immediately left everything to follow him (Mark 1:19–20). They were like the adolescent Russell: activists, engaged and confident that they could affect the world around them. They were hopeful. The particulars of their hope would need to be corrected—and paired with humility—but Jesus welcomed their hope.

The need for them to pair political hope with humility is especially evident in another story that took place during Jesus' decisive march toward Jerusalem. In Mark 10:35–45, the Sons of Thunder approach Jesus with their characteristic confidence: "Teacher, we want you to do for us whatever we ask of you" (v. 35 ESV). Jesus notably does not quash their boldness but instead engages with their hopeful desire by asking, "What do you want me to do for you?" (v. 36 ESV).

They declare their ambition. "Grant us to sit, one at your right and one at your left, in your glory" (v. 37 ESV). "Glory" in the Jewish culture is shorthand for when a divinely sanctioned leader defeats his political enemies and assumes kingship over the land. James and John have placed their hopes in Jesus, and they fully expect that his march on Jerusalem will result in victory over the current regime.

Nestled in this grand hope for victory is their own self-interest. James and John are expressing the secret (and often not-so-secret) hope harbored by countless political activists who have worked hard in a campaign. They hope that when their candidate wins—comes into "glory"—they will receive plum political appointments in the new regime, "one at your right hand and one at your left." Like Russell as a high schooler, James and John are worried that they may not get the very top spots, and so they are insisting that Jesus should promise these positions to them.

Notice that here Jesus does not rebuke them, as he did when the pair were crossing the line into political violence. Jesus does not condemn them for having hopes. Rather, he directs them toward humility. He tells them, "You do not know what you are asking" (v. 38 ESV). Jesus' assessment of them is clear: When it comes to your political hopes, your knowledge is incomplete. Your hope needs to be paired with humility.

Jesus asks a question designed to help them reflect on the possibility that they are being overconfident: "Are you able to drink the cup that I drink, or to be baptized with the baptism with which I am baptized?" (v. 38 ESV). They fail the quiz by self-assuredly replying: "We are able" (v. 39 ESV). Jesus does not condemn them for their answer but again tries to get them to realize that they are missing something important. He tells them that, eventually, they will progress to the point that they can follow in his footsteps (v. 39), hoping that James and John will pick up the logical inference that *currently* they still have a lot of room for growth.

Jesus then instructs James and John that his kingdom politics will not be defined by the pursuit of power undertaken by those at his "right or left" (v. 40). Before he can get very far, the other disciples realize and resent the fact that these two have been trying to snag political power: "They became indignant with James and John" (v. 41), and a bitter argument breaks out.

Indignation. Resentment. Conflict. When others resent your politics, pay attention. Opposition does not automatically mean you are in the wrong. Christians sometimes suffer resentment from the world because they are faithfully following Jesus. But having humility means we do not automatically assume we are in the right. Disciples are meant to continually learn. Disciples should be open—indeed, predisposed—to consider that they may be missing something important.

Sean's father, Jack, paid attention to this kind of warning sign.

When Sean snapped at his father "You're always trying to set me straight!" Sean was expressing indignation and resentment. He was offended by Jack's assumption that his political ideology was the only correct one. The force of Sean's resentment stung his dad, but Jack later shared with Sean, "That's also when I realized something was very wrong." Sean's indignation catalyzed in Jack a process of humble self-examination; it was a teachable moment that made the family's eventual reconciliation possible.

In Mark 10, Jesus turns the feelings of indignation and resentment into a teachable moment. What he teaches next are the foundational truths for a better Christian politics: "And Jesus called them to him and said to them, 'You know that those who are considered rulers of the Gentiles lord it over them, and their great ones exercise authority over them. But it shall not be so among you. But whoever would be great among you must be your servant, and whoever would be first among you must be slave of all. For even the Son of Man came not to be served but to serve, and to give his life as a ransom for many'" (Mark 10:42–45 ESV).

The politics of a Jesus disciple must look different from the world's—"those who are considered rulers of the Gentiles." Loud voices today argue that we Christians also need to play rough in politics because everyone else is doing it.

When I (Nancy) worked as a ghostwriter for political celebrities, leaders, and pundits, saw this dynamic up close. "My clients, many of whom were churchgoing Christians, did not necessarily believe that the Jesus ethic applied to politics. They were fine with using sharp elbows, slightly twisting the truth, or unfairly characterizing an event to meet their needs. When I pushed back, they called me naive. They said that the Left was playing hardball and we needed to as well, or we'd get left behind. Eventually, they got sick of me pushing back against these tactics. I quit or was fired by all of them."

Interestingly, these clients were moral in other parts of their lives. "They would never, for example, say it's okay to steal money if you were in a desperate financial situation. They wouldn't be okay with cheating on their taxes or their wives," she said. "But when it came to politics, they didn't think Christian norms applied."

When Christian politics espouse the hubris and hunger for power that characterize the standard politics of the day, something is wrong. Contemporary politics is indeed characterized by the raw pursuit of political power, where the *us* seeks to "lord it over" *them* and "exercise authority over them."

To those Christians who are drawn to adopting such tactics, Jesus responds with a stinging rebuke: "But it shall not be so among you" (Mark 10:43 ESV).

But it shall not be so among you. Jesus wants his disciples to apply humility to their relationships. Humility starts at the level of spiritual values—with the recognition that often we do not know what we are asking—and must then penetrate to the level of relationship. In the Big Shift from the *what* to the *how* of politics, we shift our emphasis from party to relationships. Instead of being preoccupied with our party coming out on top, we focus on serving others. How we relate to others must be defined by our humility. This humility isn't optional; it isn't just a tactic to employ when convenient. Humility ranks among the highest of intrinsic goods: "But whoever would be great among you must be your servant" (v. 43 ESV). Servanthood encompasses our relationships with everyone—"whoever would be first among you must be slave *of all*" (v. 44 ESV, emphasis added). "All" means all. We serve not just those on our side but also our opponents. "Us versus them" gives way to "us serving them."

Relating to our opponents with servant-like humility requires practice. Instead of serving our self-interests, we practice self-sacrifice. Serving others—including our opponents—always exacts a cost. In politics, the practice of servanthood comes with particular costs: the cost of compromise, the cost of listening to opposing viewpoints before demanding to be heard, the cost of making the extra effort to create common ground versus tearing down, and more. Jesus himself served others, even his enemies. On the cross, he "[gave] his life as a ransom for many," even for those who crucified him (v. 45). Like Jesus, his disciples pay these extra costs.

Humility does not mean that Christians should neglect advancing biblically informed perspectives in the public square on the *what* of politics. But Jesus' teaching in Mark 10 warns us that *how* we do so is of utmost importance. To repeat, Jesus did *not* say to James and John, "Whatever you do, make sure you hold the correct ideology, support the right party, and advance the correct policy." What Jesus stressed is that any political agenda must be advanced with humility and a desire to serve everyone involved.

You may think you have the absolutely correct take on immigration, abortion, police violence, support for Israel, gay rights, or any other topic. But if you are showing up in conversations without humility and without a fundamental motivation to serve everyone touched by that topic, in Jesus' evaluation you've missed the boat. Paul would reiterate this priority when he reminded the Corinthian Christians (who apparently prided themselves on their superior intellect), "If I . . . can fathom all mysteries and all knowledge, and if I have a faith that can move mountains, but do not have love, I am nothing" (1 Cor. 13:2).

On any given issue, we must ask ourselves these questions:

- Are we overconfident in believing that we alone have mastered the enormous complexity of this issue?
- Are we arrogant in claiming our desired policy is the only correct one?
- Is it possible that, like James and John, we do not fully know what we are asking?
- Are we thinking like "the slave of all" by considering the perspective of everyone—not just those on our political side?

Politicians obsessed with winning on the *what* of politics boast confidently that they know what they are asking for: "Give me your votes today, and I will guarantee a specific outcome in the next four years." The Bible reminds us that we don't even know what a day will bring forth. Proverbs 27:1 says, "Do not boast about tomorrow," and James 4:13–15 says, "Now listen, you who say, 'Today or tomorrow we will go to this or that city, spend a year there, carry on business and make money.' Why, you do not even know what will happen tomorrow. What is your life? You are a mist that appears for a little while and then vanishes. Instead, you ought to say, 'If it is the Lord's will, we will live and do this or that.'" The fact that no human knows with certainty what might happen in the next twenty-four hours should infuse all of us with humility. Russell's grandmother, for forty years, prefaced everything she ever said with "Well, if I'm living at Christmas, I think we're going to have ham."

Whether we're talking about Christmas pork or Christian politics, the Bible emphasizes that spiritual maturity means understanding that you do not know everything, and you could be wrong, so tread carefully.

This intellectual humility should translate into a relational humility that practices servanthood for the common good. "We don't know everything" should flow into "It shouldn't be all about us." Evangelicals today are widely perceived as practicing self-serving politics—just like James and John. For example, we are inconsistent when applying our own principles: we will insist on civil liberty and freedom of expression when our rights are being infringed, but we are quick to censor and punish when those same rights are being exercised by *them*.[1]

Invariably, when one subgroup—whether on the Right or the Left—pursues power solely for self-serving aims, they inevitably cause resentment among everyone else. Just like the Sons of Thunder triggered the indignation of their peers, Christian politics today has the same effect on many of our non-Christian neighbors. It is having the same effect on our children.

Children of adult evangelicals increasingly perceive their parents' political behavior as overly self-confident and self-serving. They associate their parents' lack of humility with their parents' churches, which is contributing to what researchers have called "the Great Dechurching." Sixty-eight percent of dechurched evangelicals said their parents had something to do with their departure from the church. They cited as key reasons their parents' overemphasis on the culture wars, inability to listen, unwillingness to engage other views, problematic attitudes on race, and lack of love, joy, and generosity.[2]

Now is our teachable moment. Our politics must make the Big Shift. We are called to reflect our Lord, the one who "came

---

1. David French, "Free Speech for Me but Not for Thee," *Atlantic*, April 11, 2022, www .theatlantic.com/ideas/archive/2022/04/republican-dont-say-gay-bill-florida /629516/.
2. Jim Davis, Michael Graham, and Ryan P. Burge, *The Great Dechurching: Who's Leaving, Why Are They Going, and What Will It Take to Bring Them Back?* (Grand Rapids: Zondervan Reflective, 2023).

not to be served but to serve" (Mark 10:45 ESV). If we hope to preserve this nation and our faith for the next generation, we must grow our humility.

DOES HUMILITY WORK?

Critics will attack the vision of political humility depicted in Mark 10:42–45. They won't do so by providing an alternative biblical interpretation of this seminal teaching on politics by Jesus. Rather, their argument is ostensibly practical: political humility just won't work, at least not in our contemporary context. They contend that American evangelicals are so oppressed politically that we cannot afford to practice self-denying servanthood today like the disciples did in their day. To get a sense of this type of argument, google "Christianity is under attack." Plus, you might receive fundraising emails from your favorite pundits or organization using this line of panicked reasoning to separate you from the money in your wallet. After all, it's much easier to get donations if there's an impending emergency. These critics attempt to pit hope against humility: if we hope to win (or even survive), we must sacrifice humility and fight, fight, fight.

There are several ways to respond to this argument. We could start by comparing the religious liberty and political power enjoyed by American evangelicals to what Jews were suffering under the Roman regime. The notion that we have it so much worse today and therefore cannot afford the political humility commanded by Jesus in his day is simply untenable. Against much worse odds, the early Christians followed Jesus' model of self-sacrificial servanthood of others. Hopeless? The early church's willingness to serve everyone (especially the most vulnerable, whether they were Christian or not) stood out as a compelling witness born out of the teachings of Jesus and ended up transforming the entire Roman Empire.[3]

We could offer rebuttals from our own nation's political history. For instance, there is the 1960s civil rights movement. The harsh realities of Jim Crow oppression of Black Americans make the complaints of White evangelicals seem puny. Yet Dr. Martin Luther King Jr. and other Black Christian leaders based their political strategy on the cost-bearing servanthood of Jesus. Hopeless? No. Akin to the early church, this movement successfully achieved stunning and unprecedented political and cultural change in the United States.

Humility can lead to hopeful outcomes. Research has consistently shown that expressions of humility are highly persuasive in political debates.[4] Curtis, David, and Russell have all engaged in real-world politics, and we have experienced

---

3. Rodney Stark, *The Rise of Christianity: How the Obscure, Marginal Jesus Movement Became the Dominant Religious Force in the Western World in a Few Centuries* (San Francisco: HarperCollins, 1996); C. Kavin Rowe, *Christianity's Surprise: A Sure and Certain Hope* (Nashville: Abingdon, 2020).
4. Francesca D'Errico, "Humility-Based Persuasion: Individual Differences in Elicited Emotions and Politician Evaluation," *International Journal of Communication* 14 (May 2020), https://ijoc.org/index.php/ijoc/article/view/11477/3107.

the profound difference between these two approaches when applied to politics. A *how* of politics that mirrors Jesus' hope and humility will stand out in the world and have a positive impact. It features listening instead of lecturing; moral consistency instead of hypocrisy; compromise instead of power plays; caring about the common good instead of pursuing narrow self-interest; and us serving them instead of us versus them.

Will this approach always win? Will it always work? The answer depends on how you define "win" and "work." Christian hope means trusting in God's timeline, not our own. His finish line and final judgment of history will take place on a schedule that far exceeds our short lives. Christian humility means trusting that God is in charge, not us. When that final evaluation occurs, we will discover just how much God's definitions of "win" and "work" exceeded our limited conceptions.

Hope and humility. These were the spiritual values that defined Jesus' march to Jerusalem toward the cross. Hope and humility must define how disciples follow in his footsteps now.

THE FOUR PROFILES

Let's return to the Hope/Humility conversation starter.

What was your profile outcome?

Your profile places you somewhere on the following quadrant:

Let's dive a bit deeper into each of these profiles.

Combatant

The Combatant profile is high in hope and low in humility. Combatants are fighting political battles because they believe their side can win. But their fighting spirit is untempered by the possibility that they do not know what they are asking. They believe confidently that their side is right, and that's that.

We may see this among uncompromising young activists with sweeping policy demands, overzealous parents at a PTA meeting, or that one person who dominates conversations about politics. They engage because they believe their world can improve, but they miss the complexity of an issue or the validity present in opposing views.

In politics, Combatants exercise a level of influence that greatly exceeds their numbers. This is because politics, like any human activity, is dominated by those who care the most. And out of all the profiles, the Combatants care the most about winning. For them, the stakes are very high.

Picture the Combatant as the one who has their fists up to the world. They are more than ready to engage, but their posture means they are also defending themselves against any countervailing influence.

Exhausted

The Exhausted profile is the negative-photo image of the Combatant. The Exhausted is low in hope and high in humility. This profile is essentially humble: the Exhausted do not claim to have all the answers. They fear that no one can figure a way out of the current conflict and so have given up on politics entirely.

We see this exhaustion among people skipping family reunions riven by partisan conflict, blocking anyone posting politics on social media, and changing the subject whenever this topic comes up in conversations. When conflict arises, they want to back away into the bushes.

In America, surveys show that this profile is more widespread than any other profile, giving rise to the term "Exhausted Majority." Compared to the Combatants on both sides, the Exhausted Majority holds more moderate views, are more open to compromise, and dislike the spirit of hatred overtaking politics.[5] But the Exhausted exercise much less influence than would be warranted by their numbers.

---

5. Stephen Hawkins et al., *Hidden Tribes: A Study of America's Polarized Landscape* (New York: More in Common, 2018), https://hiddentribes.us/media/qfpekz4g /hidden_tribes_report.pdf.

The reason is obvious: you cannot exert influence when you are hiding in the bushes.

Picture the Exhausted as the ones who have their shoulders slumped and their faces buried in their hands. In their politics, though they are not offending or hurting others, they are squandering their potential influence for good.

Cynic

The Cynic profile is low in both humility and hope. Like Combatants, Cynics believe they are right and are not really open to learning otherwise; unlike the Combatant, the Cynic is especially self-convinced about one particular truth: things are hopeless. Like the Exhausted, the Cynics have given up—but unlike the Exhausted, the Cynics are so certain of their stance that they influence others with their deep-seated pessimism.

In their combination of certitude and disengagement, Cynics can seem sophisticated (indeed, for many Cynics, this is part of the appeal of this posture). Their disengagement makes their critical takes more convincing than those of Combatants, who can be more easily dismissed as biased. As confident and seemingly sophisticated critics, Cynics often exercise social influence disproportionate to their numbers.

The long-term effect of the Cynic is corrosive, however. At the individual level, cynicism is self-corrosive: this posture leaves the holder stewing in a spiritually degrading mix of pride and despair. At the broader societal level, the spread of the "I know better" and "everything is hopeless" combination corrodes our institutions. Institutions depend on people trusting institutional knowledge. But as more citizens are influenced by the self-certitude of cynicism, the average person is increasingly willing to believe that he—armed with a few online videos produced by fringe voices (that sound very confident)—knows better about the complexities of specific issues than the established scientific institutions. Institutions also depend on the participation of people. As politicians cynically undermine trust in our political institutions, however, people feel that any kind of engagement is hopeless; many don't bother to vote, much less pursue more active engagement.

Picture the Cynic with arms folded, eyebrows slightly arched, standing above it all. In his politics, he is not offering his own constructive energy; he is only proffering critiques that tear down what is around him, especially the institutions that affect so much of our lives.

Disciple

The Disciple profile is high in humility and hope because Disciples have submitted their political lives to Jesus. Disciples are humble: they recognize that the political world is defined by complexity, and this means that there are rarely obvious and easy answers. Disciples believe firmly in objective truth but are much less firm that they themselves have complete ownership of truth. The Disciple thus is willing—eager, even—to listen and learn from others, including others who might hold different views.

The Disciple is also filled with hope. The Disciple believes that Jesus is the Lord, the King of Kings. She has faith that Jesus will ultimately restore all of creation—including the political world—to God's loving and just purposes. The Disciple places her hope for this final restoration in Jesus and his final return, not in human political parties or leaders. In the meantime, the Disciple seeks to serve the world by acting as a signpost to that ultimate hope.

Picture the Disciple as the one whose head is inclined forward seeking to listen and learn, and whose arms are held open ready to accept and serve.

All of us leading *The After Party* long to grow toward being more faithful Disciples. And we need to keep growing spiritually. We know so much about the Combatant, Exhausted, and Cynic because they describe us, the leaders of *The After Party* project. David identifies with the Combatant, Russell with the Exhausted, and Curtis with the Cynic. Each of us will have more to share about our profiles in the coming chapters.

While we will recount how we are seeking spiritual growth from our various starting places, you will learn to hear from God about your own individual journey. The Bible is full of such personalized invitations from God. Paul was fighting as a Combatant when Jesus shocked him on the road to Damascus (Acts 9:1–9). Elijah was slumped as the Exhausted one on Mount Horeb when God's still, small voice whispered to him (1 Kings 19:11–13). Thomas was standing apart as a Cynic when the resurrected Jesus came looking specifically for him (John 20:24–31).

God will find you, wherever you are on the map.

The advantage of the Hope/Humility quadrant is that everyone can find their place on this map and potentially meet others who are different in ideology, party, and policies. Republicans and Democrats alike are found among the Combatant, the Exhausted, the Cynic, and the Disciple. People within the same quadrant may differ on the *what* of politics, but they share a common spiritual journey on the *how*.

On this map, different profiles can also potentially help each other. For instance, the Exhausted can absorb some hope from the Combatant; the Combatant can learn some humility in the other direction; the Cynic can glean from both. All are united by Jesus' invitation to change our posture, to become more like the Disciple, whose head is inclined forward seeking to listen and learn, and whose arms are held open ready to accept and serve.

What if the Hope/Humility exercise revealed that you already can be categorized as a Disciple? Well, you probably still have room to grow. You can also serve those around you.

Jesus' Great Commission to his disciples is to go and make more disciples (Matt. 28:16–20). Read the rest of the book as a way to better understand your friends and family members, and how you can—with hope and humility—help them grow toward better Christian politics.

REFLECTION EXERCISE

1. Record your profile here: _____.

2. How do you feel about your political profile? Circle which of these possible responses might apply to you (you can circle more than one):

Seen	Hesitant
Affirmed	Confused
Emotional	Annoyed
Raw	Frustrated
Curious	Angry

3. Be curious.
   a. Even if you are not sure you agree quite yet with the profile assigned to you, put it on for size for a moment. How might this profile

provide further insights about how you engage in politics?

b. This profile refers to your posture toward politics. But do you see this posture in other parts of your life as well? If so, how?

4. Understand others. Look at the other profiles that do not describe you.

a. How do you feel about the other profiles?

b. Do the other profiles describe people you know?

c. Do they describe anyone on your "disappeared" list?

d. How might this profile help explain them?

CHAPTER 3

THE COMBATANT

A QUICK REVIEW

We all start somewhere on this Hope/Humility graph, and no matter where you begin, moving toward being a Disciple requires growing in hope and humility.

Combatants start out low in humility and high in hope: they are sure they are right and can help their side win. Their spiritual growth means focusing on growing their humility. If you match this profile, this chapter is for you.

If you are not a Combatant, reading this chapter will still help you understand what is happening in Christian politics. Recall that the combination of low humility with high hope gives the Combatant outsize influence in politics, because, compared to the Exhausted and the Cynic, they are the most engaged and energized. Therefore, regardless of your profile, you are being influenced by the Combatant. The Combatant may be that friend, relative, or church member who has directly created distress or perhaps even disappearance in relationships.

Indirectly, the Combatant mindset has so thoroughly shaped contemporary American political culture that we are all relating to this profile in one way or another.

To get started, let's hear from *The After Party*'s resident Combatant.

DAVID'S STORY

My dad was a math professor, and his college students sometimes came to the house to visit. Even though I was only eight or nine years old, I would sit with history books in my lap and ask the students to come talk to me. My goal was to teach these college students about the nuances of the Revolutionary War.

I had definite opinions on just about everything, especially history. And this tendency did not abate as I got older. If my high school classmates could sum up my personality in one phrase, it would be "ready for debate."

I've always instinctively gravitated toward conflict and am drawn to the fray. While I was always conscious of the need to be kind, I have to confess that for far too long in my life I prioritized the quest for justice over kindness and humility. I believed if I expressed any doubt about my own positions, I was expressing weakness. In many ways, I formed friendships in spite of these characteristics, not because of them.

When I became a litigator, all of these habits were reinforced. I would minimize the flaws not just of my paying clients but also of the people I considered friends or allies, and I magnified the failings of the opposing parties on cases and of my partisan political opponents in debates. It happened so naturally that it took me years to realize that adopting this mindset outside of courtrooms (which are designed to accommodate debate and are carefully shaped by rules of evidence) constituted a form of bearing false witness. I was regularly creating a false picture of friends and enemies alike.

I'd like to say there was a specific moment when I understood my own mistakes and repented of them.

But the reality is that I changed slowly in response to experience. My humility increased the more I learned.

I cringe at the memory of some of my past arguments—for example, about race and policing. I spoke with great confidence in spite of what I now know was the most surface knowledge. The more I learned, the less confident I became in what was a standard conservative position.

Time and again, the more I learned, the more I regretted my previous combativeness. I was trying hard to win arguments, when I now realize I wasn't even right. I see myself when I see some of the sharpest voices online, and I offer a silent prayer of thanks that Twitter or X did not exist when I was in law school.

As a result, I have a high degree of compassion for people who are drawn to conflict. I understand that instinct.

I also know it takes time to grow out of the worst versions of yourself.

THE PARTISAN MIND VERSUS THE MIND OF CHRIST

David's story explains why it is so difficult for the Combatant to move out of his quadrant. The operating system of the Combatant is the partisan mind, which redirects all new information into the us-versus-them framework, such that "Us is right (and indeed righteous); Them is wrong (and in fact, evil); and Them is out to get Us (so we better fight back with everything we've got)."[1]

When the Combatant is a Christian, the partisan mind can be especially powerful. This person believes not only that *us* is right but also that *us* is on God's side.

When I (Nancy) was a ghostwriter, I attended a political presidential rally in 2016 with one of her clients. The rally began with an opening prayer asking God to grant victory to this presidential candidate. "Dear heavenly Father, we come confidently before you," the preacher prayed, "because we know that [this candidate's] righteous goals for America line up with your Word."[2]

It is easy to believe (at least in politics) that an individual and God are of one mind. Armed with this mental equation, the Combatant feels little motivation to leave his quadrant: moving toward greater humility seems like spiritual weakness, a compromise with evil, and foolishness. Here, then, is the key biblical truth for the Combatant: a partisan mind and God's mind are not the same. The partisan mind is actually opposed to the mind of Christ.

God's own mind is revealed most completely in Jesus Christ. Modern evangelicals attempt to apply the mind of Christ on perplexing individual decisions, much like the old

---

1. For an excellent overview of the social-psychological dynamics in this kind of thinking, see Jonathan Haidt, *The Righteous Mind: Why Good People Are Divided by Politics and Religion* (Vancouver: Langara College, 2020).
2. Nancy French, *Ghosted: An American Story* (Grand Rapids: Zondervan, 2024), 195.

WWJD ("What would Jesus do?") campaign. But in the early church, the concept of the mind of Christ was originally developed to correct a larger-scale problem: group divisions where the us-versus-them mentality had taken root.

The apostle Paul consistently refers to the mind of Christ to address such divisions within the church. When Paul wrote his first letter to the Corinthians, the church had been split into rival camps formed around different personalities. Each faction was asserting superiority and dismissing the others. Paul diagnosed anyone fighting in this manner as "the person without the Spirit [who] does not accept the things that come from the Spirit of God but considers them foolishness" (1 Cor. 2:14). He called his audience to instead grow toward becoming "the spiritual person" who has "the mind of Christ" (vv. 15–16 ESV). Guided by the mind of Christ, the spiritual person—the Disciple—will adopt humility in his dealings with others.

In his letter to the Philippian church, Paul encourages Christians to "make my joy complete by being like-minded, having the same love, being one in spirit and of one mind" (Phil. 2:2). What defines that "one mind"? Paul makes it clear in the next verses:

> In humility value others above yourselves, not looking to your own interests but each of you to the interests of the others. In your relationships with one another, have the same mindset as Christ Jesus:

Who, being in very nature God,
>   did not consider equality with God
>   something to be used to his own
>   advantage;
>   rather, he made himself nothing
>   by taking the very nature of a servant,
>   being made in human likeness.
>   And being found in appearance as a man,
>   *he humbled himself*
>   by becoming obedient to death—
>   even death on a cross!

—PHILIPPIANS 2:3–8, EMPHASIS MINE

Paul is repeating Jesus' teaching on political humility to James and John in Mark 10. The fact that Paul is applying that same teaching to his different audience is significant. Paul is the apostle to the Gentiles, charged by Jesus himself to take the gospel beyond the confines of Israel to the nations. This means that Jesus' insistence on humility is not confined to the particular political divisions within ancient Israel that motivated James and John (e.g., Zealots versus tax collectors). Political humility is an essential and universally applicable aspect of the gospel itself. Wherever the gospel goes, political humility comes along as part of the package deal. The mind of Christ inherently overturns all versions of us versus them—all expressions of the partisan mind—in all places and in all times.

The letter to the Colossians presents the most sweeping depiction of how the mind of Christ can transform the partisan mind of the Combatant. Colossians begins with the breathtaking declaration that, in Jesus, "all the fullness of God was pleased to dwell, and through him God was pleased to reconcile to himself *all things*, whether on earth or in heaven, by making peace through the blood of his cross" (Col. 1:19–20 NRSV, emphasis mine). "All things" means just that: the reconciling scope of the cross encompasses all ideologies, all parties, all policies (the things composing the *what* of politics). All things are transformed "by making peace through the blood of his cross," which means that all relationships broken by the *what* things of politics are meant to be restored via the *how* spiritual value of peace.

Of course, people can choose to reject Jesus and opt out of this comprehensive reconciliation offered by God (Col. 1:23). People can reject the cross. But even their rejection does not alter God's invitation to all humanity that encompasses all aspects of life, including politics. Even to those who currently refuse him, God extends the same invitation of reconciliation.

Reconciliation to God inherently leads to reconciliation with others. This cannot be emphasized enough. Because all things that divide us from God are meant to be transformed into reconciliation, all things that divide us from each other are also meant to be similarly transformed. As people are reconciled with God through the cross, they inevitably must become reconciled with each other around the cross. The cross expresses God's intention that there should no longer be any us versus them. God desires only one *us*, gathered around Jesus by the reconciling power of the cross

There's one party, and everyone's invited.

As all Combatants draw near to Jesus' party, they will necessarily bump shoulders with their perceived enemies, just like Simon the Zealot and Matthew the tax collector had to sit at the same dinner table. Colossians draws a straight line from the reconciliation of all things to God (in 1:20) to the reconciliation of the major social hostilities dividing the Greco-Roman world: "Here there is not Greek and Jew, circumcised and uncircumcised, barbarian, Scythian, slave, free; but Christ is all, and in all" (3:11 ESV). This list of opposing pairs is meant to convey the universal and timeless power of the cross to reconcile all divisions in all times, and we can certainly add to the list Right and Left, Republican and Democrat, conservative and liberal.

As the cross has made peace in the "us versus God" conflict, so it must make peace in all human us-versus-them conflicts. The two reconciliations are inseparable. To insist on combat against *them* is to insist on combat against God.

This means that the Combatant wishing to enter Jesus' party must check at the door a forbidden weapon: the partisan mind. Colossians 3:2 explains that we all must redirect our minds to seek what is above from God and reject previous patterns of thinking.

By the way, what will be a sign that the partisan mind has

been left at the door? Ancient texts reveal that those us-versus-them divisions listed in Colossians 3:11 (e.g., Greek versus Jews) were marked by hostile speech. Each side trash-talked, belittled, mocked, and spread rumors about the other side—much the same way today's partisan Combatants do. The Jesus party does not allow for such verbal practices. This is why a verse prior to Colossians 3:11's sweeping declaration of social reconciliation includes a very practical description of the required change in speech: "But now you must put them all away: anger, wrath, malice, slander, and obscene talk from your mouth" (Col. 3:8 ESV).

How do you describe your political opponents? Is your speech marked by anger, wrath, and malice? For all of us, we will know we are growing spiritually when we talk about *them* differently, when hostile speech is replaced by humble speech. This takes time. Colossians 3:9–10 describes the transformation of speech as an ongoing process: "Do not lie to one another, seeing that you have put off the old self with its practices and have put on the new self, which is being renewed in knowledge after the image of its creator" (ESV). Notice again how the change in practices ("do not lie to one another") is interconnected with ongoing transformation of one's mind ("being renewed in knowledge after the image of its creator").

Let's now explore how Combatants can transform our minds so that we can be renewed in knowledge after the image of our creator.

DAVID'S STORY

To understand better my ongoing transformation from Combatant to Disciple, let's return to my decision to go to Iraq and what I learned there.

In October 2005, I was president of a small civil-liberties nonprofit located in Philadelphia. I was thirty-six and living in an apartment with my wife, Nancy, and our two kids. I supported the war in Iraq. I didn't really have any kind of national voice, but—to the extent my opinion mattered—I voiced it loudly and vociferously. Saddam Hussein had to go. You know the rest of the story. We toppled his regime in a lightning war but then faced a grinding insurgency. By late 2005, the Sunni-Shia civil war raged, American casualties mounted, and the army struggled to meet its recruiting targets. Who wanted to fight and die in what seemed like a losing war?

One evening, at home in Philadelphia, I read the story of a marine officer who had been wounded in Anbar province. He'd used a reporter's satellite phone to call his wife and two kids to tell them that he was hurt but he'd be okay. At that instant I was hit with a burning sense of conviction. How could I support a war I wasn't willing to fight in?

With Nancy's blessing, I enlisted. I walked to the recruiting office in downtown Philly and asked about getting an age waiver and joining the army JAG Corps. I almost flunked my initial physical. I was so nervous my blood pressure spiked. I tried to run myself back into shape but pulled a hamstring on my first jog. Let's just say I wasn't the most impressive person in officer basic training at Fort Lee, Virginia. I didn't have an infantry body, but I did have a legal mind. So I offered what I had. Everyone called me "Professor" (I'm a former Cornell Law School lecturer), and the drill instructors seemed to delight in saying to me things like "Professor, get in the plank position," or "Professor, drop and give me twenty."

In June 2007, I volunteered to go to Iraq. Before I left, I spoke at a conservative convention in California about my religious-freedom legal work. Someone in the crowd raised his hand and asked a question about my upcoming deployment. "Well, with you doing all of this important work here at home," he asked, "why would you go abroad?"

"The two greatest threats to America are far-Left radicals at home and jihadists abroad," I said. "And I feel called to fight both." The crowd applauded, and I felt pretty good about myself.

By November, I was at Forward Operating Base Caldwell in Iraq with the Third Armored Cavalry Regiment. While serving in the eastern Diyala province in the heart of the Sunni insurgency in the middle of the Sunni-Shia civil war, I saw the most dreadful sights that still haunt me today. Under al-Qaeda's thumb, this was one of the deadliest places on earth. I saw atrocities. I saw genocide. And seeing these horrors made me realize I had been afflicted with a partisan mind, and I had afflicted my partisan mind on others.

I was ashamed that I'd told that California group that I was committed to fighting "far-Left radicals at home and jihadists abroad." What an inaccurate, disparaging comparison. I am embarrassed that I compared my political opponents at home with these people who were every bit as vicious and brutal as ISIS became in the ensuing years. I experienced what it was like living amid jihadists who ended up killing many of my friends.

As much as I disagree with university radicals, I lived a happy life in law school in deep-blue Cambridge, Massachusetts. My son was born in deep-blue Ithaca, New York. I lived comfortably on the outskirts of Philadelphia's so-called gayborhood. While I could easily live with liberals, frankly the idea that I would use these far-Left radicals and jihadists in the same sentence was embarrassing. I had to repent of that and ask for forgiveness, because the comparison I'd made was wrong. I now seek to leave behind the partisan mind. It's not just that I recognized greater complexity during my deployment, it's that I gained greater clarity about my own fellow citizens.

My roommate Captain Leo Broadhead played a key role in helping me see other perspectives. Staff officers lived and worked in the same building. With four men in my room, everything was remarkably cramped. The late evenings often represented a peaceful respite (except for the outgoing artillery fire). For me, after harrowing days spent grappling with matters of life and death, I blew off steam by arguing with Leo about politics. Leo was our unit's liberal Mexican American Mormon-Catholic-agnostic adjutant, and his perspective could not have been more different from mine. I grew up as a Christian from the cradle and was from rural Kentucky. Leo was from Wisconsin and he scoffed at religion. As a former Mormon and former Catholic, he told me he belonged to the "church of the Hubble telescope" because he believed only what he could see and it "sees farther than us all."

We served together during the surge, and from November 2007 until I deployed back home in September 2008, I heard him talk about Barack Obama almost as much as he talked about his wife (just kidding, Sandra!). I couldn't count the number of religious, political, or other arguments we'd had in the course of more than three hundred days of living together. Hours and hours of debate wouldn't budge him one inch from his wrongness.

We didn't change each other. He didn't become like me. I didn't become like him. But he was my first friend in Iraq. I don't think I've spent more time under more stress in a single year with any person alive, including my wife. One of Leo's most powerful acts of friendship was going to chapel with me, every week, even though he didn't believe. I didn't ask him to go. He just went. He went because friends do stuff together—and the greater the challenges confronting us, the more the word "together" matters.

No matter what our political affiliation, we were brothers. Both conservative soldiers and liberal soldiers fought jihadists, side by side.

Now that I'm home, why would I think I'm at war with them here? I disagree with the Left and much of the populist Right, vigorously. If and when any of my political opponents seek to undermine our fundamental freedoms, I'll be there to pick a legal, political, and cultural fight with them. But I won't turn my back on the truths of Scripture. I won't stop seeking justice, loving mercy, and walking humbly. No political "emergency" justifies rejecting the mind of Christ and biblical truth.

Leo helped me recognize that my political opponents were my neighbors. They were also my brothers
in arms. When I wore the uniform of my country, I was
willing to die for them. I served next to them, even
though my band of brothers was all over the political
spectrum.

When Leo redeployed back home, I used some
law-school connections to get him prime seats at
Obama's inauguration. How did Leo reward me for
this act of generosity? By sending me a video of him
flipping off George W. Bush's helicopter leaving the
White House while he sang the "Goodbye Song."

I wouldn't have wanted it any other way.

REFLECTION EXERCISE

1. Identify a story in your life when you finally
    discovered you were wrong about something
    important. The story doesn't have to be about
    something political, per se; it could be
    • how you handled a relationship,
    • some disagreement at work,
    • a financial decision,
    • or anything else that felt important at the time.

In free-write form (where you just start writing and don't stop, letting the words come to you), reconstruct this story from memory.

2. Reflect on the period in the story *before* you discovered you were wrong—the part of the story when you felt like you were right.
   a. Why did you think you were right?
   b. What were you feeling during this period? (Example emotions could include anger, disdain, pride, or confidence.)
   c. What do you regret about this period?

3. Identify the process by which you discovered that you were actually wrong about this issue. How did this discovery happen?
   a. Was it something you did differently?
   b. Was it somebody else doing something differently?
   c. Was it the world revealing truth differently?
   d. Something else?

4. As you reflect on that story, what wisdom do you want to take from it and apply to how you relate to others around politics?

THE GIFT OF THE COMBATANT

Does the prospect of checking your partisan mind at the door make you feel like you're being asked to lose your very personality? If Jesus' party is to be marked by peace, reconciliation, and unity, the Combatant may wonder, "Where is my place in all of this? Am I not wanted or needed? Is the Jesus party just for 'softer' personality types?"

We get why you are feeling this way. As Combatants, we can care so much about politics that we become our partisan identity. Our very minds become fused with the partisan mind. Losing our partisan mind can thus seem like we are losing our minds, losing ourselves.

But the true essence of the Combatant is not the partisan mind. The partisan mind is actually a distortion of God's intended design for the Combatant personality.

David exemplifies this truth. When considering David's many virtues, his friends would especially name courage and steadfastness. David is willing to take a stand and stick to what is right. These are core virtues of a prototypical Combatant; indeed, they led David to volunteer to serve in an active combat zone in Iraq. As David began to heed Jesus' invitation to leave behind his partisan mind in politics, he didn't lose any of these virtues. On the contrary, as David explains, "As I became more of a Disciple and less of a partisan Combatant, I became a better version of my true self."

Jesus wants—and needs—the Combatant to bring his or her true self to his party. To understand why, let's turn to the book of Ephesians. The first half of the book revolves around the vision of reconciliation identical to that in Colossians. Ephesians also explains how the cross makes peace between us and God and must lead to making peace between us and them: "But now in Christ Jesus you who once were far away have been brought near by the blood of Christ. For he himself is our peace, who has made the two groups one and has destroyed the barrier, the dividing wall of hostility. . . . His purpose was to create in himself one new humanity out of the two, thus making peace, and in one body to reconcile both of them to God through the cross, by which he put to death their hostility" (2:13–17).

Peace, unity, reconciliation, ending hostility—at first blush, Combatants may hear this as the soothing background music for a gentle party that doesn't need them.

But then in Ephesians 6:11–12, we hear a very different tone struck. Listen closely to this passage: "Put on the full armor of God, so that you can take your stand against the devil's schemes. For our struggle is not against flesh and blood, but against the rulers, against the authorities, against the powers of this dark world and against the spiritual forces of evil in the heavenly realms."

"Put on the full armor," "take your stand," "struggle": these notes sound like the hype music for a big boxing match!

What's going on? How do these two invitations belong to the same party?

The answer is found in the key line "For our struggle is not against flesh and blood." The partisan mind misdirects the virtues of the Combatant to fight against flesh and blood—the people on the other political side. The true enemy is "the devil's schemes." The higher spiritual plane—not the lower levels of human ideology, party, and policy—is where the most crucial fight takes place. The Christian vision of reconciliation is not a soft avoidance of any conflict but rather involves fighting the real battle: "against the spiritual forces of evil in the heavenly realms." The core strategy of the devil's scheme is to sow division and hostility between people.

Why is this? As Ephesians 2 explains, reconciliation between people divided by social and political lines demonstrates the power of the cross. What better way for the devil to discredit the power of the cross than by re-creating those very conflicts?

A high-stakes battle is underway. Right now. But the struggle is not against flesh and blood: it is not Right versus Left, Republican versus Democrat. The battle is against the devil, the Evil One who seeks to undermine the credibility of the cross's power to "reconcile all things." The devil is trying to pit people against each other via politics. The devil especially loves to foment political hostility among Christians, as this undermines the credibility of the cross.

To combat the devil, we need Combatants with all their

God-designed virtues to join the fray. This is why the very next verses in Ephesians continue to sound the battle cry: "Therefore put on the full armor of God, so that when the day of evil comes, you may be able to *stand your ground*, and after you have done everything, to stand. Stand firm then, with the belt of truth buckled around your waist, with the breastplate of righteousness in place, and with your feet fitted with the readiness that comes from the gospel of peace" (Eph. 6:13–15, emphasis mine).

We need the courage and steadfastness of the Combatant to help Christians stand their ground. But that ground is not marked by the dividing lines of ideology, party, or policy. That ground is not a battleground against other people, against flesh and blood, against *them*.

Where are Christians to plant their feet? We take our stand with our "feet fitted with the readiness that comes from the gospel of peace."

We make our stand for peace, God's peace. Right now, it is far, far easier to be carried away by the tidal waves of political hostility. It takes no courage to participate, as long as you go along with your political tribe's version of us versus them. But try calling your political tribe to all that is involved in the "gospel of peace"—to reconciliation, truth, complexity and humility, abstention from angry and malicious speech—well, you will need all the true virtues of the Combatant to take that spiritual stand. You will then be fighting against the true enemy: the devil and his dark forces.

The courage required in this true battle was powerfully demonstrated by the 1960s civil rights movement. Chicago pastor Rev. Dr. Charlie E. Dates recounts how this movement fought for racial reconciliation. This fight was rooted in the biblical vision of the one *us*, a vision that went from the cross all the way back to the beginning in "the scriptures where God made all of humanity in His image and His likeness: we are image bearers, and therefore we have and we maintain an essential dignity given to us by our creator."[3] This fight required courage of the highest order, taking a stand in the face of attack dogs, bombings, lynchings, and more.

Reverend Dates points out that the Christian leadership of the movement, with Dr. Martin Luther King Jr. at the fore-front, understood that they were fighting a spiritual battle, not one against flesh and blood: "It was not necessarily Black versus White so much as it was right versus wrong." The movement was founded "not as a simple us versus them," he explains, but rather as a struggle against "the forces of evil at play, at war against the forces of good."[4]

This movement, born out of a Christian worldview that bravely fought this spiritual battle against the devil's attempt to divide Americans along racial lines, achieved amazing progress in dismantling Jim Crow—although much still needs to be

---

3. Quoted in session 3 of *The After Party* six-week video course. For information on the course, see https://redeemingbabel.org/the-after-party.
4. Quoted in session 3 of *The After Party* six-week video course.

done in the area of racial justice. We can forget how miraculous its achievements are. At the outset of the movement in the 1950s, most political commentators believed that its vision of transforming centuries of racial segregation was hopeless.

What gave this movement the hope to fight this seemingly hopeless battle? Dr. Dates gives the only answer that makes sense: "It was a visit of the Spirit of God, because of the preaching that restored the dignity of a people downtrodden for hundreds of years. This Spirit reignited their belief and their confidence that they could face oppression and opposition. The movement had to be truly empowered by the Spirit of God."[5]

When things seem hopeless, the Spirit of God is drawn to those who can still access hope. This is why in our current moment, when our political polarization seems so hopeless, the Spirit of God is drawn to the Combatant. In the Hope/Humility quadrant, out of the three profiles en route to the Disciple, the Combatant is the one who enters with the most hope.

If you are a Combatant, the rest of us need you to do the spiritual work of checking your partisan mind at the door, because we need you. Your hope—newly redirected away from short-term partisan victory instead to the lasting peace of God—is a much-needed gift to the Jesus party.

Will you bring it?

---

5. Quoted in session 5 of *The After Party* six-week video course.

REFLECTION EXERCISE

1. Identify a situation in your life where you see the us-versus-them mindset dominating. It could be a situation about politics, per se, but it could be some other kind of division (in your neighborhood, school, extended family, church, etc.).

2. Put on the "mind of Christ" and imagine Jesus entering this situation.
    a. What would Jesus hope for? How would he express his hope?
    b. How would Jesus "fight" to achieve this hope? What would that Jesus fight look like?
    c. What costs would he have to be willing to bear?
    d. How would his intentions require courage?

3. If possible, locate a fellow Christian who has not taken one side or another of this particular situation.
    a. Share your reflections from question 2 with this person.
    b. For the next week, meet with this person (in person or virtually) and together pray for ten

minutes about this situation. Together, ask specifically for Jesus to share with you the "mind of Christ."

c. And then see what happens!

CHAPTER 4

THE EXHAUSTED

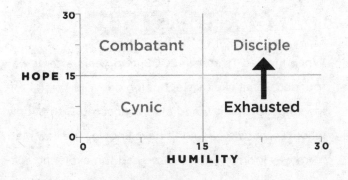

A QUICK REVIEW

The political future of our nation and our church depends, to a great extent, on the Exhausted. That's a heavy load to put on a group that already feels tired, but it's true. The "Exhausted Majority" represents the largest numbers of Americans overall and Christians in particular. They represent the most potential for healing because they already possess a spiritual value much needed in politics: humility. The problem is that the Exhausted feel too drained to bring their best selves into the political realm. And the spiritual value that has most drained from their souls is hope.

How can the Exhausted grow in hope? This is the move that takes a person in this profile toward the Disciple, and this chapter will explore how this can happen. To grasp the opportunity for growth, however, we need to first understand how the Exhausted got so drained in the first place. This story from *The After Party* project's resident member of the Exhausted category sheds some light.

RUSSELL'S STORY

When I joined Twitter in 2008, two years after it was founded, it felt like the technological Wild West. I followed people I knew and also connected with people whom I otherwise wouldn't have known. The new platform was invigorating, and we had fun exploring, joking, and laughing together in 140 characters or less.

But just two years later, in 2010, it changed for me. I remember the moment. I was hanging out with my friend who had just written a popular book about living for Jesus instead of pursuing wealth and comfort. On Twitter, I posted that we were together and joked about how we were driving around in his new Bentley.

That evening, back at home, I went online. Anyone

who knows me, or this author I was with, would know we were not cruising around in a $250,000 car. But the backlash on Twitter was immediate and decisive: "How could a person who just wrote a book against materialism drive around in an expensive car?" one user demanded in a typical response to my tweet. There were accusations of being tone deaf, insensitive to the impoverished, and more.

And with this, Twitter changed for me. What had originally been the technological Wild West became the O.K. Corral—a location of daily shootouts. And people, at least rhetorically, were shooting in my direction.

I don't like fighting, but I've noticed that some people are invigorated by it. I've gone to people's homes for dinner where the husband and wife fight like cats and dogs for five minutes over something trivial and then—as if nothing had happened—simply pivot back to the meal.

"Well, this is just how we talk to each other" or "We love it," they might say. "Pass the potatoes, please."

But arguments make me look for the nearest exit.

And as Twitter became more and more toxic, I was firmly ensconced on a social media platform where people were constantly criticizing and provoking me. I wasn't sure how to handle a platform that seemed engineered to exhaust users. When we post something and others like it, this creates a little hit of dopamine. But, like anything else, we need more and more of it in order to get the same result. And being on a hamster wheel of approval seeking is the best-case scenario with any of the social media platforms.

Yet often we don't get any approval from others, which skews how we perceive everything. When we don't get the response we want on a post, we might conclude nobody cares about us. Other times, we get attacked over a post and feel like everybody hates us. Neither of these is true, but it certainly feels like it.

I had a primal response to social media. Every time I checked my mentions, my anxiety skyrocketed. It was like walking into a dark house not knowing if there was something there ready to jump out at me. Social media led me to a place where I was constantly on guard looking around for a possible attack. When I couldn't monitor it, it made me feel uneasy and vulnerable.

This toxicity exhausted me, and I lost the ability to maintain attention. I always needed to know what was going on. If I was on a plane that didn't have wifi, I'd stare at the tray in front of me wondering what I was missing. *Oh wait*, I'd think. *I don't know what's going on*. I developed a siege mentality. I began to think that everybody was out to get me, and the least I could do was pay attention to the attacks.

It was enough to make me want to take a break—a real, intentional break—from the constant barrage of developments, outrage, and trivia in our never-ending news cycle.

I needed to leave it all behind, and I knew just the place.

I'd lived and worked in Louisville, Kentucky, for sixteen years. During that time, I would often take an afternoon and drive down past Bardstown to one of my favorite quiet spaces on the planet—to Abbey of Gethsemani, the Cistercian monastery made famous by writer Thomas Merton. There, I could find the quiet I needed to pray as I walked around the hills in rural Kentucky, alone. Sometimes I would sit in the unnervingly quiet chapel there to collect my thoughts, especially when I was trying to make a big decision.

During all the Twitter hysteria, I made that drive again. I wanted to spend time in prayer and refocus my life. But now, unlike during my seminary years, I had a phone. There in my pocket. Beckoning me, warning me, demanding my attention.

In the quiet at the abbey, my eye caught a light reflecting in the glass on the other side of me. When I looked up, I could see that the reflection was of me—or, rather, of my phone awakening with notifications. I had gone to the monastery to get away from everything.

But there in the quiet, when I was supposed to be praying, I kept thinking about Twitter. I felt vulnerable because I didn't know what was being said on the app.

Suddenly, instead of praying, I started checking my Twitter feed.

The first thing I thought about in that flash of recognition as I held my phone was not Gethsemani but Gethsemane: *Could ye not tarry with me one hour?* What had happened to my attention span, and to my priorities, that I could not endure the silence for more than a few minutes without "checking in" with what seemed more pressing, more "real"? I slipped the phone into my pocket, but I was exhausted by my own inability to concentrate on why I came, so I gave up and left the monastery.

THE SOCIAL MEDIA DILEMMA

Is your social media experience similar to Russell's story? If so, it's not surprising. Social media is uniquely affecting, and here's why:

- The business model of social media companies is to gain your attention at all costs, so that you will view their ads.[1]

---

1. Sean Illing, "There's a War for Your Attention. And You're Probably Losing It," *Vox*, November 17, 2016, www.vox.com/conversations/2016/11/17/13477142/facebook-twitter-social-media-attention-merchants.

- Content that triggers negative emotions—such as fear, anger, disgust—is a proven and powerful method of gaining initial clicks.[2]

- For Russell and people like him, seeing such content creates an ambivalent reaction:[3] they feel compelled to click initially but then drained by the feelings engendered.

- Thus, to gain the next click, social media algorithms are built to ratchet up the fear, anger, and disgust, which creates the next ambivalent response cycle of compelled/exhausted, which signals the social media algorithms to boost the next dosage, and rinse and repeat.[4] The neurological result is the classic addiction loop that Russell described.

- Additionally, the business model of social media is built on sorting people into identical groupings, so that it can feed content particularly targeted at those groupings. Social media mirrors the Big Sort, replicating online what is already happening geographically. The various tribal definitions of *us* are being fed alarming depictions of *them*, and the chasms widen with every click.

---

2. Claire E. Robertson et al., "Negativity Drives Online News Consumption," *Nature Human Behaviour* 7, no. 5 (2023): 812–22, https://doi.org/10.1038/s41562 -023-01538-4.

3. Ofir Turel and Hamed Qahri-Saremi, "Responses to Ambivalence toward Social Networking Sites: A Typological Perspective," *Information Systems Journal* 33, no. 2 (2022): 385–416, https://doi.org/10.1111/isj.12407.

4. This dynamic was also depicted in the documentary *The Social Dilemma* (2020), directed by Jeff Orlowski.

There is debate about whether social media creates new polarization or mirrors existing divisions. "I think it's absolutely a part of the story, but it's also easy to overread the influence of social media," says David. "I'm not positive about this, but I'm pretty sure that Twitter was in its infancy during the Civil War, and we had no problem going at each other on the battlefield, pre social media." But even if social media is better understood as a mirror, it is one of those carnival mirrors that grossly exaggerates things—especially as it magnifies despair.

In the past, people used to hear about events that pertained only to their lives. In *Amusing Ourselves to Death*, Neil Postman describes how, if someone you knew died, you might be told in person about the tragedy, and you could then bring food to the bereaved or help in other ways. People received information about events that mattered to their lives, over which they had some degree of control.

But the advent of the telegraph allowed people to learn information about faraway incidents over which they had no control and for which they could offer no help. In addition to local news, hometown newspapers began covering national and global events as well.

"The local and the timeless . . . lost their central position in newspapers, eclipsed by the dazzle of distance and speed," writes Postman. "Wars, crimes, crashes, fires, floods . . . became the content of what people called 'the news of the day.'"[5] This gave people a sense of helplessness, since they couldn't do anything about the tragedies they encountered in the news.

"We desensitize ourselves to suffering," writes Tish Harrison Warren, "because we are overwhelmed by the scale of world-wide suffering. We are small people who, for the most part, live quiet lives, but we have access to endless stories of pain and brokenness."[6]

This constant exposure to news also affects our political perceptions.

In 1968, for example, the United States suffered from massive civil unrest and experienced much political violence. Sometimes there were two or three domestic terror bombings per day right here in the USA. But if you were living in Montgomery, Alabama, and a mail bomb went off in Topeka, Kansas, you would never know it. It would not appear in local papers and would not have been a significant-enough news story to edge out reporting on Vietnam. But now, if a kid gets his MAGA hat knocked off in a Burger King in Des Moines or another kid gets coffee spilled on her BLM shirt, hundreds of thousands of people can be upset over it on social media.

---

5. Neil Postman, *Amusing Ourselves to Death: Public Discourse in the Age of Show Business* (New York: Penguin, 1986), 66–67.
6. Tish Harrison Warren, "A Life of Prayer amidst News of Death," InterVarsity Women Scholars and Professionals, August 14, 2014, https://thewell.intervarsity.org/blog/life-prayer-amidst-news-death.

All of these individual incidents, even in the aggregate, don't add up to the same level of political violence we had in 1968. But because social media alerts us to these incidents, we have a feeling that there's more violence and unrest. The feeling that *us* is being threatened by *them* gets reinforced more constantly now than in the past. This creates a heightened sense of political dread and fear that's unique to this modern technology.

The end result is exhausting. And it is especially exhausting because many of us feel trapped in front of this carnival mirror. Many readers will nod along with this analysis, agree how awful social media is, and take a break from reading this book to go check their Instagram feed. All of us leading *The After Party* project struggle with our own ambivalent feelings about social media. You sense the nature of this ambivalence when you see someone post something political in nature, become ensnared in a back-and-forth flame war, get exhausted and declare "I'm taking a break from social media," and go silent, but then a few months later they are back on the addiction loop. Rinse and repeat.

Calling Christians to resist social media feels analogous to asking them to resist the Big Sort. The sociological forces acting on us are enormous. And just like there are probably good reasons to stay located in your politically homogeneous neighborhood, there are good reasons to stay connected to others via social media. We want to hear about the new jobs, the birthdays, the graduations, the births.

It's not all political toxicity, all the time.

Social media is not all bad, and we don't have all the answers on how to stem the effects of social media on our lives. But we do believe that the Exhausted need not and should not remain hopelessly trapped in the very practices that drained them in the first place. You can move toward hope.

HOPE AND SOCIAL MEDIA

The first steps involve grasping the biblical understanding of hope—a rich topic that has been explored by the greatest Christian thinkers—and then applying this understanding to our social media practices. Here is our definition of biblical hope: creating signs pointing toward God's future. It's important to underscore how different this definition of hope is from a more popular conception of hope that could be characterized as merely wishing things will get better.

Creating signs pointing toward God's future involves action: it is like going out and buying a new outfit and a hostess gift because you fully expect you're going to get invited to an awesome party this weekend and want to be ready. Compare that to the popular version of hope, which is akin to sitting alone in your apartment wishing someone would invite you to a party.

Hebrews 6:11–12 warns against associating hope with passivity: "We want each of you to show this same diligence to the very end, so that what you *hope for* may be fully realized. *We do not want you to become lazy*, but to imitate those who through faith and patience inherit what has been promised" (emphases added). First Peter 1:13 reinforces that our active participation is required to direct our minds toward God's promised future: "Therefore, preparing your minds *for action*, and being sober-minded, *set your hope* fully on the grace that will be brought to you at the revelation of Jesus Christ" (ESV, emphases added).

Social media may have certain benefits, but it cannot grow our biblical hope. The medium inherently puts us in the passive mode where we place ourselves at the mercy of its algorithms to feed us whatever it calculates. Our passive disengagement is a central draw of the medium. This is why we scroll to disengage from work, the people around us, or our true selves when discomfiting feelings of emptiness and boredom arise.

In contrast, biblical hope that creates signs toward God's promised future frequently leads us to engage with discomfort. In perhaps the most beautiful New Testament passage about hope, the apostle Paul declares, "Not only that, but we rejoice in our sufferings, knowing that suffering produces endurance, and endurance produces character, and character produces *hope*, and *hope* does not put us to shame, because God's love has been poured into our hearts through the Holy Spirit who has been given to us" (Rom. 5:3–5 ESV, emphases mine).

Growing in this kind of hope—that kind that engages us in suffering the way Paul describes—simply cannot happen via social media. Social media plays to the generic hope of merely wishing things will get better. We are drawn to our feeds in hopes of getting that short-term dopamine hit that comes with some post that momentarily surprises, delights, or amuses us. We want to be distracted from discomfort, not led through it. We are lured to keep wishing (and scrolling) for more pleasant distractions, because social media keeps us off balance by mixing in the dopamine hits with adrenaline surges of fear; the fear is often political in nature and conveyed by posts warning of the latest ways that they are out to get us. Overall, this creates that social media experience described by Russell as "walking into a dark house and not knowing if there's something there ready to jump out at you."

We need to grasp one more aspect about why biblical hope cannot grow via social media itself. To repeat, hope is creating signs pointing toward God's future. The pivotal event in God's future is our "blessed hope—the appearing of the glory of our great God and Savior, Jesus Christ" (Titus 2:13). In chapter 6, we'll unpack more about this future event and its implications for today's politics, but for now it is critical to emphasize that this return of Jesus is an in-person event. His second coming will not happen on Zoom; it won't be announced via a viral video. Jesus will come back in his resurrected body, and he will resurrect our bodies, and we will reunite with him and with others in person via our new bodies.

Jesus created an enduring sign that points toward the

embodied nature of God's ultimate reunion: the shared meal. Luke 24 tells two wonderful stories of Jesus doing this. First, he appears to two disciples on the road to Emmaus. The two have been doing the ancient equivalent of scrolling through their news feeds: they were absorbed in "talking with each other about all these things that had happened" (v. 14 ESV). As the three of them walk, Jesus begins to reshape their understanding by teaching them. But the process is not completed with just sharing more information. Jesus stays with them until they invite him to a meal, and he breaks bread with them. The shared meal is the moment they truly recognize Jesus, as "he was known to them in the breaking of the bread" (v. 35 ESV).

In the very next story of Luke 24, Jesus then appears to the other disciples. These disciples undoubtedly also have been absorbed in rehearsing the recent events of the crucifixion and fearing they will be persecuted next. They are jumpy and easily startled. Jesus wishes to address their emotional state, asking them, "Why are you troubled, and why do doubts arise in your hearts?" (v. 38 ESV). He first offers them empirical evidence from his very body, showing them his hands and his feet (v. 40). But just like with the two other disciples on the road to Emmaus, Jesus knows that sharing evidence is not enough to address the emotional state of his disciples. He next asks: "Have you anything here to eat?" (v. 41). It's a question that seems like a complete non sequitur—unless one recognizes how the shared meal is central to Jesus' transformation of anxious disciples. The act of eating together is what leads to the opening of their minds (v. 45).

The shared meal was Jesus' sign that God's future will also be an embodied enjoyment of a restored world, one where he will repair all broken things, people, and relationships. This is why Jesus commanded that all disciples regularly re-create this sign in what we call Eucharist (or Communion). God's future is best envisioned as a dinner party.

And this is the final reason why social media, by itself, cannot grow our true hope. Posting pictures of the dish we just ordered for others to see (and perhaps envy) is not remotely akin to the wedding feast of the Lamb, to which we are all invited (Rev. 19:9). We can create signs pointing toward God's future only when we are engaged with each other in embodied and in-person form.

What, then, do we do about social media, especially in our current political context? Minimally, Christians should be handling their social media lives with a core spiritual practice that the Bible outlines for any activity prone to addiction: namely, the practice of fasting.[7] In particular, we would all

---

7. For more on this topic, we recommend two books by our friend, Christian thought leader Andy Crouch: *The Tech-Wise Family: Everyday Steps for Putting Technology in Its Proper Place* (Grand Rapids: Baker, 2017), and *The Life We're Looking For: Reclaiming Relationship in a Technological World* (New York: Convergent, 2022).

   The following is not a Christian book, but it is a helpful work of social science (the author is a professor of sociology at Duke University): Chris Bail, *Breaking the Social Media Prism: How to Make Our Platforms Less Polarizing* (Princeton, NJ: Princeton University Press, 2022).

   Additionally, this article might help you think about social media fasts: Kevin

do better—emotionally, relationally, physically, and especially spiritually—if we spent considerably less time on social media and traded that time to be with other people in person, preferably while sharing meals together. And even better for our hope, we should be doing so sometimes with people who are otherwise suffering alone. That is how the Exhausted will renew their biblical hope, as they create such signs of God's future.

Are we willing to make this trade? It is part of the Big Shift from being preoccupied with ideology, party, and policy disputes on social media to embracing the spiritual value of hope, engaging in relationships and adopting corresponding practices. If we are willing to make this trade, to make this Big Shift, a big payoff awaits us. Not only will we moderate our exposure to emotionally draining news on social media, but we will also gain the opportunity to actually redeem the (hopefully limited) time we do spend on these platforms.

How so? Well, imagine a new practice that informs how disciples of Jesus use social media. This new practice is not lazy and passive consumption but an imaginative and proactive invitation. Imagine a social media practice that enacts the parable of the master's great banquet in Luke 14. In that parable, the master throws a great feast, but his original guests do not properly value his invitation. So the master commands his servants, "Go

---

DeYoung, "Why You Should Consider a Social Media Fast," *Gospel Coalition*, November 28, 2012, www.thegospelcoalition.org/blogs/kevin-deyoung/why-you -should-consider-a-social-media-fast/.

out quickly to the streets and lanes of the city, and bring in the poor and crippled and blind and lame" (v. 21 ESV).

The great banquet is a picture of God's great future. Wouldn't it be motivating to be his servant, creating signs pointing toward this future? And wouldn't it be wonderfully redemptive if social media could be how we "go out quickly to the streets and lanes" to find the guests that most need to hear God's invitation?

NANCY'S STORY

I have a story that shows how this can happen.

When I was a kid, I was sexually abused by a preacher after vacation Bible school.

I didn't talk about this very much. Most people knew nothing about it. I was able to partition this off from my life as "something bad that happened" and "something that was not okay." I didn't want to be known as a victim, so I didn't bring it up. I immersed myself in church and the GOP—people who loved God, promoted "family values," and valued marriage. I was a Republican during Bill Clinton's administration, and I appreciated the moral clarity that the GOP, evangelical Christians, and other conservatives had about his sexual predation.

In 2016, I was a ghostwriter for Republican politicians, as ensconced in the GOP as a person can get.

But I was alarmed when I saw how my fellow conservatives waved off Trump's predatory comments and the many credible allegations of abuse and rape that later emerged.

I mentioned this to my counselor, who encouraged me to write about my own abuse as well as how the modern moment made me feel. The goal was to come back the following week and hand him my story, and we could go from there. (This would prevent me from having to go through all the details verbally, which I was still not ready to do.)

I went to Waffle House and drank hot coffee while I typed a screed against Hillary Clinton and Donald Trump. "The first female president possibly will have ridden the coattails of her husband (who has been accused of rape) to the Oval Office," I wrote. "And the GOP nominee who likes younger women used to hang out with a known pedophile and bragged on video about doing to women what the preacher did to me so many years ago."

I was dismayed by how both Democrats and Republicans responded to sexual abuse, but my real beef was with the Republicans. I expected more of them. Of us.

By the time I closed my laptop at Waffle House, I'd decided I would not simply hand this over to my counselor the following week. I would publish it in the

Washington Post. I knew evangelicals would not like the piece, but I didn't expect the ways some of them responded.

Over the course of the next few days, some conservatives said I was sanctimonious and untrustworthy. They said I let my personal experience cloud my political judgment. A conservative journalist characterized my victimization as "screwing around with her preacher," and that horrific lie spread all over the internet. People began calling me the "seducer of pastors," and some speculated that David and I had a Black child not because of international adoption but because of infidelity. They made racist memes of our family, taking photos from my Facebook account. They made pornographic images of me.

This sort of humiliating online sexual harassment was especially devastating to me as an abuse survivor. I'd been pushed out of my political nest. I was in free fall.

On social media, I'd had enough of following those accounts where the person had a Bible verse in their profile description while they were lying about me. In the past, I generally followed people who were ideologically similar to me, but now I valued kindness above every other metric. I began to like and follow anyone who was nice. One New Yorker—her handle indicated her name was Kathy Kattenburg—expressed support. Her profile did not include a photo but had a meme that read "I Stand with Immigrants." After I followed her, however, I saw her tweets and how she often interacted with others in cruel ways—especially my husband. When David posted on Twitter, Kathy was there to disagree, challenge, and even insult him.

When David posted about the Second Amendment, she accused him of supporting laws that would kill people. If he posted about biblical sexual beliefs, she mocked his "archaic" beliefs. If he posted about class warfare, she replied, "Wow. This is a truly awesome pity party." When he wrote about his faith, she replied, "Pushing God on suffering human beings as a cure for their problems is incredibly offensive." When he wrote about false sex-abuse claims, she accused him of promoting "rape apologists." When he wrote about education, she accused him of being "misleading," "deeply antidemocratic," and "reflexively hostile to America." When he posted against anti-Semitism, she wrote, "David, stick to bemoaning antichristian attacks on 'orthodox Christian sexual morality' & leave the definition of anti-Semitism to ppl who know what it is." On other posts, she wrote, "It's a shame that u don't know what the word 'fact' means," or "This is nonsense," or "As a lawyer, u should know better."

She was most angered when he expressed pro-life

views. David had been a pro-life attorney for decades and had created the first pro-life club at Harvard, and Kathy didn't like that. She posted frequently about her multiple abortions and stridently attacked pro-lifers.

Since David liberally muted accounts, he never saw these tweets. I didn't unfollow Kathy but neither did I trust her. I kept her at a digital arm's length. This went on for four years.

In March 2020, everyone was in duress because of COVID. All over America, food services were overwhelmed by orders, grocery stores had limited options, and everyday items were impossible to obtain. That's when I noticed a tweet from Kathy: "I am alone in this apartment. I envy people who have families so much," she wrote. "I feel hopeless. I will never have food. Never."

I knew this was a plea for help, but I didn't immediately act. I mulled over whether I should reach out to this total stranger. I knew I should, but I really didn't want to. She seemed to hate our values, she definitely hated David, and I wasn't even sure she was a real person.

About an hour later, however, I messaged her. "Are you having trouble getting groceries?"

I soon discovered she was a disabled woman living alone in a greater New York City area walkup. Because millions of people were relying on the same food services, her normal grocery delivery had been disrupted.

She'd paid money for her food but it hadn't been delivered. Since her grocery money was tied up, she had no way of affording other food even if she could figure out a way to obtain it.

"I've not been able to get groceries for weeks," she messaged me.

My heart sank. This was a bad situation for anyone, and I knew I should try to help.

But living in Tennessee, I had no idea how to get food to New York. At the time, I was busy helping my own aunt and parents by going to the store and shopping for them, but they lived only a few miles down the road. "I can at least try to help," I promised.

"Really? You would help me?" She sounded genuinely grateful but also surprised. "Can we talk on the phone?"

I paused. A phone call felt intrusive and worrisome, since I had no idea what sort of person would have dedicated herself so thoroughly to trolling my husband. I imagined it could go poorly, and she would tweet out that she finally had connected to the French family and we were as awful as she feared. I wondered if she would record it and confront me.

On the slim chance I could locate food during the pandemic, I needed to figure out what she needed. I took a deep breath and sent her my phone number.

When it rang, my heart sank. What was I getting myself into? Why had I even reached out?

In her accent—pure New York—she commented on my Southern drawl. "I have to say I was surprised you reached out."

"Me too."

Her phone persona was much different from her online persona, but I was still suspicious. I was talking to someone who had dedicated a great deal of time to mocking David for beliefs that I held too. This would not end well, but maybe it would be okay if we steered clear of any meaningful conversation.

"Listen, I know this is unusual for you and me to be on the phone," she said. "But I've been eating pancake mix for several weeks, and it's about to run out."

I liked her cutting to the chase. We would not be friends, but maybe we could obtain food. "If I can figure this out—a big if," I said, "what do you need?"

We made a list: toilet paper, diced tomatoes, Aldi chimichangas, bananas, along with other food requests. My heart softened as she told me how much she loved those chimichangas. Though I'd suspected she was a bot, she was a real person who loved Aldi. That detail broke me. Online, she was so sure of herself, so confident, so brutal—but right there on the phone she was admitting that she needed help. She did so in the most vulnerable and beautiful way, which was happening only out of necessity. If it weren't for the pandemic, we never would've spoken.

Armed with Kathy's grocery list, I attempted to send food to her. I placed another order with Instacart, even though it was backed up and unreliable. Then I placed an order on Amazon, which had just announced they would be prioritizing food deliveries. In both cases, however, the need was too great. The groceries would not come for weeks.

Since Kathy was Jewish, I contacted various synagogues near her, but they weren't able to help. I was Presbyterian, so I contacted various churches around her as well. Same story. Would I need to drive from Tennessee to New York with a trunk full of food?

A day passed. Then another. We talked every day, her hunger and mood worsening. I hoped one of my orders would come through, while Kathy continued to eat her ever-dwindling supply of pancake mix. Three days passed without any food appearing at Kathy's apartment. Every day, we talked on the phone with updates.

"We're no closer to getting food," I said. "I don't know what to do." We sat in silence.

"The only thing I know to do is pray," I finally said. This was sort of a platitude—I was trying to indicate that this effort was out of our hands, that we needed a miracle. But Kathy surprised me. "Okay, go ahead."

"What?" I asked. I never pray with anyone, and I certainly did not expect this person who had trolled David for years based on his faith-informed political reasoning to agree to pray with me. Wasn't one of her critiques of David that he allowed his religious views to seep into his political views? I didn't have the luxury of thinking about all of that in the moment. "You mean, you are up for praying with me right now?"

Even though I had asked her to pray, I wanted to back out. I felt that praying with her was way too intimate, too vulnerable, like I was opening myself up to more criticism. "To be honest, I'm not sure how Jews pray," I admitted. "I don't want to offend you. Is it all the same, just not in the name of Jesus?"

"Pray however you want," she laughed. It was a rare moment of levity, as Kathy's mood had darkened with each passing day without additional food. And so, right there on the phone with this stranger, I prayed—awkwardly—"Dear God, please help Kathy to get food before the pancake mix runs out."

The next day, I contacted a friend in New York for advice. She suggested hiring a person to physically go to the store for Kathy and deliver her groceries to her door. Using this service, I found a shopper and talked her through Kathy's grocery list—coffee, cornflakes, blueberries—as she walked through the aisles of Aldi. "Don't forget the chimichangas!"

An hour later, Kathy called me. This was four days into our quest for food, and two weeks after her food supply had gotten thin. But this time, when the phone rang, I was not filled with trepidation. I knew, or at least hoped, this would be good news.

"You wouldn't believe what's here!" She was laughing and crying at the same time as she described being surrounded by bananas, cereal, toilet paper, beef, and chicken. A few hours later, another grocery honored our previous order and she got another load of food. Double of everything.

"How can I eat fourteen bananas?" Kathy laughed. But she managed. She had enough freezable and fresh food so she could eat well until the grocery services had time to catch up.

But by this time, Kathy and I had talked every day for a week. We'd bonded over this strange, COVID-catalyzed effort to find food, and we stayed in contact. We finally had an honest conversation about the trolling, which she told me she regretted.

"I still don't agree with anything David writes," she said, "but he can't be all bad if he's married to you." She told me she was sorry for all she had written about him, and even vowed to give David the benefit of the doubt.

After her pantry was full, she sent me photos of the recipes she was making with her new abundance of food. When I went on walks, I sent her photos of my path to enjoy since she couldn't get out of her apartment. When I discovered she enjoyed reading, I sent her some of my favorite novels, which we read together and discussed. We talked about books and God, and even watched a sermon together and talked about the differences between Christianity and Judaism. I asked her about her abortions, and she asked me about my faith. So much for keeping Kathy at arm's length. We became friends and kept in touch for years.

Neither of us have caused the other to change a single political position. I loved Kathy Kattenburg, however, and she loved me. I could tell she still found David's political writings baffling, but she no longer wrote derogatory things about him online. Instead, she respectfully disagreed.

That was years ago, but we still keep in touch. Recently, on a trip to New York, David and I stopped by Kathy's place, and we walked to a pizza place at the foot of her building.

Though it was difficult for Kathy to navigate the stairs and make that journey, David offered his arm and we slowly walked to the diner. When we finally arrived, it was fun to be able to sit with both David and Kathy—former enemies—and laugh about all we've been through together. She is now, against all odds, a part of our family, and our meal was shared slices of pepperoni and cheese.

REFLECTION EXERCISE

- Review again your list of disappeared ones. Focus on the people who live nearby. Pray and ask God to lead you to someone who elicits a sense of longing for a further reunion (this could be someone whom you've already chosen for a previous exercise, or it could be a new person).

  Write this person's name: _____.

- If you and this person are both on social media, review his or her posts to see what has happened in this person's life in the following categories:
  - Cause for celebration
  - Cause for congratulation
  - Cause for sympathy
  - Cause for prayer intercession
  - Cause for meeting a concrete need

- Pray for this person at least three times along these lines, and jot down what the Holy Spirit stirs within you.

- Consider sending a message (perhaps via social media) expressing celebration, congratulation, sympathy, or some other positive sentiment. If you feel comfortable, share that you have been praying for this person. If so, write down the response you receive.

- Depending on the response, consider a way that you can bring a shared meal into the picture. Perhaps it is offering to bring them home-cooked or store-bought food in a time of stress or need. Perhaps it may even involve offering to take them out to express celebration, congratulations, or sympathy in person.

- If you are going to meet in person over a meal, here are some suggestions:
  - Stay away from politics for this first engagement.
  - Have in mind a short list of things you know are happening in his or her life (because you've seen references to them on social media) that have sparked your curiosity. Come ready to listen.

- Come with a short list of things happening in your own life that you are willing to let the other person in on. Be ready to share about those things.

CHAPTER 5

THE CYNIC

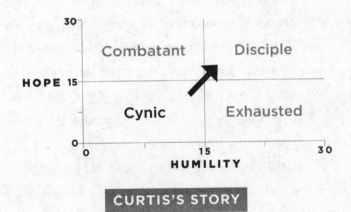

"Come on, really?" Russell tilted his head in disbelief. "You're the Cynic?"

I was having a cup of coffee with Russell early in our project planning, discussing which quadrant of the Hope/Humility scale applied to each member of our team. He readily saw that David was the Combatant and he was the Exhausted. But initially, he wasn't buying my self-identification with the Cynic.

People might initially conceive of a Cynic as someone devoid of morals or prone to manipulation. I'm glad that Russell doesn't view me as that kind of person, and I like to think he's right. But there's a way to locate the Cynic via the more subtle categories of the Hope/Humility graph, and based on this definition, I think I really do qualify.

The Cynic is low in hope and low in humility. Like the Exhausted, Cynics are prone to feeling that the political world is hopeless; like Combatants, they are sure they are correct in their views. This combination puts Cynics in a posture of detached judgment: they are sitting it out (because it's all so futile) with arms folded and one eyebrow arched (because they think they know better than those still engaged).

Both Russell and David had been heavily engaged in the political sphere for years, but I had studiously avoided this world for most of my adult career. But I rarely admitted to anyone else—and perhaps even to myself—the real reason: I was a closet Cynic.

My avoidance wasn't for lack of interest in politics. Like Russell, as a young boy I dreamed of growing up to become the president of the United States. As a nine-year-old, I used my own money to purchase a weekly subscription to *Time* magazine and devoured every edition front to back. On my own, I practiced public speaking to hone the oratorical skills that would advance my presidential candidacy. Like Russell, I started out high in hope.

But I discovered the limits to my aspirations in this country. In my junior-high civics class, I read about article 2, section 1 of the Constitution, which states that only natural-born citizens are eligible to become president. I immigrated to the United States from Taiwan when I was three years old, so I was disqualified.

A bit disappointed, I shifted my hopes a few spots lower in the constitutional hierarchy. I fixated on a figure that had appeared on multiple covers of *Time*: Henry Kissinger. Despite being an immigrant himself (from Germany), Kissinger had risen to the powerful positions of secretary of state and national security advisor in two Republican administrations in the 1970s. Since my role model was a Republican, I adopted his party identification as my own. In the 1980 presidential election (the first one about which I remember having formed thoughts), my teenage self was drawn to the optimistic persona of Ronald Reagan. I imagined my adult self as the Asian American Kissinger in a future Republican administration.

While my hope levels remained high, I have to admit: I was also drawn to Kissinger's vibe that no one would have characterized as "humble." In public appearances, Kissinger carried himself as if he were the smartest guy in the room, the one who knew it all. I was drawn to his sense of intellectual self-confidence that bordered on—and probably often crossed over into—arrogance. I wanted to be him: the guy who saw the world more deeply than everyone else. I entered college with high hope and low humility.

In the first month of my freshman year, I met some Black Christian undergraduates who invited me to a weekly Saturday morning study group. I had grown up in a quasi-fundamentalist church that entirely avoided any teaching on politics. My new friends were the first Christians I had ever met who were trying to dig into Scripture to excavate the connections between faith and politics.

They believed the central connection between these two realms was justice. The group opened my eyes to how much Scripture calls us to "do justice" (Mic. 6:8 ESV). As Black Christians, this meant paying attention to racial injustice. Each Saturday morning, we pored over Scripture and American history, and connected those insights to our experiences as people of color—all with an eye toward excavating racial injustice. Every week was filled with intellectual and emotional discoveries. Hearing the traumatic stories of my Black friends reawakened painful memories of my own immigrant experience. For instance, I remembered how often, during elementary school recess, White classmates would pull their eyes into a slanty shape and shout, "Ching Chong Chang!" I started to wonder if I had been incredibly naive as a child in thinking that I could have had a shot at being accepted as a national political figure.

Over the next few years, I kept digging. I sought out the mentorship of a Black sociology professor, who also was a Christian. He taught me that underneath everyday experiences of racism are less-visible structural barriers: laws, economics, social dynamics, and politics that historically have barred people of color from everyday opportunities to own homes, build wealth, live free from fear of police brutality, and other basic rights enjoyed by Whites. The rosy view of America that I'd had as a young Reagan Republican began to darken. In my foreign policy classes, I also began to learn about the devastating impact of Kissinger's foreign policy during the 1970s that included indiscriminate bombing of Asian countries such as Cambodia and Laos. As an Asian American, it struck me that Kissinger would never have ordered the equivalent actions in any White European country.

As I uncovered this ugliness, I experienced an emotional dynamic I've since noticed in many people who want to cling to a high level of hope in their politics. When people place hopes in the *what* story of politics—a particular ideology, party, policy set—they are vulnerable to disillusionment. Political ideology, party, and policies are human constructs. If we dig deeply enough into those human constructs, we inevitably discover human fallibility and sin. Previously rosy views darken and former heroes fall. When people like me experience our first version of this disillusionment, we do not necessarily shift our hopes to an entirely different kind of story, like the *how* story of politics emphasized by Jesus. Instead, we stay in the *what* story of politics but swing over to the other ideological side, thinking that is where hope can still be found.

That's what I did. My political ideology swung way over to the left side of the ideological spectrum. I helped create a new political coalition of Asian, Black, and Hispanic student groups, and we launched a campaign for a new policy of minority-faculty hiring on campus. I pinned my hopes on the progressive version of the *what* story with this new set of ideology, party, and policies.

Some people can sustain their levels of political hope by making this kind of switch. This happens in

both ideological directions: I've met my share of disil-
lusioned former progressives in the conservative political ranks. But I could not sustain my hope in this
way. Once I got in the mode of digging for the ugly
and dark realities underneath any political story, I
couldn't stop.

Inevitably, I began to encounter failures in my new
tribe. Cynicism has an acidic quality: it corrodes whatever it touches, regardless of the particular *what* of
politics. The longer I spent on the progressive side, the
more I felt like I was uncovering its hypocrisies. I especially disliked the way progressives promoted themselves as the party of "tolerance" while being very
intolerant of orthodox Christianity. Progressives de-
nounced authoritarian regimes abroad but enforced
domestically a kind of soft totalitarianism on views
about gender and sexuality.

I even grew increasingly uncomfortable with the
progressive tendency to overplay the "race card" and
to make blanket denunciations of America. Yes, my
classmates had taunted me on the playground, but
that same school system also gave me enormously
better opportunities than I would have had in Taiwan.
I still believed in opposing racism and injustice, but I
felt that the story of America nevertheless could not
be reduced to those realities. For all its faults, America

still enjoys more racial diversity than any other nation, and I'd still pick America over any other option. I came to believe the progressive dogma of identity politics was limiting and even self-defeating for the very racial groups being mobilized. Would it have really served a teenage Curtis to believe that America is hopelessly racist and everything is stacked against me?

My cynicism about both sides contributed to my eventual abandonment of political engagement. I first went into ministry and then later shifted careers to start a management-consulting firm serving secular non-profits. Politics was hopeless. I was staying out of it.

This sentiment grew in 2016, when I watched what happened to David. He and I had become friends through a fantasy baseball league in grad school (which has continued through the decades to this day). By 2016, David and Nancy were calling out the political hypocrisy on the Christian Right: for example, how the same people that condemned Bill Clinton's lack of character and mistreatment of women were now rushing to justify Donald Trump. I witnessed first-hand how David endured vicious attacks on him and his family. While I expressed sympathy to him and to Nancy and appreciated their courage, I also heard that Cynic voice within me: "See, it's hopeless. I know better than they do. I'm not getting involved."

JONAH, THE CYNIC

"It's hopeless. I see more deeply than others. I know that underneath all is just ugliness. So I'm sitting it out." This is the posture of the Cynic, a combination of low hope and low humility, which results in judgmental disengagement. It is a posture depicted by biblical characters as well.

Let's turn to the story of Jonah, an Old Testament story we usually tell to children to delight them with the "in the belly of a fish" episode. But the entire narrative is actually a profoundly nuanced depiction of the spiritual and political journey of the Cynic.

The political dimension is established in God's initial call to Jonah. God commands Jonah to "Arise, go to Nineveh, that great city, and call out against it, for their evil has come up before me" (Jonah 1:2 ESV). Nineveh is the capital of the Assyrian Empire, the hated enemy of Israel. While the exact timing of the story is unclear, the fact that the city is in its state of greatness means Jonah hears God's call either after Assyria has already wiped out the Northern Kingdom of Israel or is threatening to do so. In the us versus them of Israel's international politics, Assyria is the ultimate *them*. Jonah has plenty to say about "their evil [that] has come up." It is quite possible that the Assyrians have already slaughtered or kidnapped Jonah's friends and relatives.

But he does not want to deliver God's message to them

on their turf. One probable reason is that Jonah believes he is going to get slaughtered. Jonah believes he is going to get viciously attacked by his political enemies the moment he opens his mouth. In response to God's command, Jonah thinks: "No, thank you—I know better. It will be hopeless to try to speak directly with the Assyrians."

This combination of low hope and low humility leads Jonah "to flee to Tarshish from the presence of the LORD" (v. 3 ESV). Tarshish lies in the opposite direction from Nineveh, which indicates Jonah intends to avoid this assignment. But the Lord will not let his cynical prophet go that easily. He sends a storm to frustrate Jonah's escape plan, and Jonah recognizes that God is pursuing him. Rather than turn around and face the Lord, Jonah tells the sailors to throw him overboard into the raging sea.

Jonah sinks into the deep waters. What will he discover there? Chapter 2 shifts into poetic form, signifying that his physical descent is meant to convey spiritual depth. Even though Jonah went overboard alone, he narrates the act in terms of an encounter with God: "For you cast me into the deep, into the heart of the seas, and the flood surrounded me; all your waves and your billows passed over me" (2:3 ESV).

What do we discover as we go deeper and deeper into the world? The Cynic believes the deeper you probe into the world of politics, the worse it gets. You'll just discover more pain, hypocrisy, sin, and ugliness.

As Jonah sinks into the depths, he thinks he will sink so deep that he will be "driven away from your sight" (v. 4 ESV). Instead, he discovers that God still hears him in the pit of his despair: "When my life was fainting away, I remembered the LORD, and my prayer came to you, into your holy temple" (v. 7 ESV).

In the depths, God hears and saves. His power is embodied by the giant fish that swallows Jonah and holds him for three days in its belly. This strange rescue conveys an important spiritual truth: God's rescue of the Cynic does not involve making all the ugliness and pain disappear. A three-day stay in the innards of a fish is not a luxury hotel vacation. Imagine the smell of the intestines, the heaving motions, the constricted pressure of the tight space. Jonah describes his experience as being in "the belly of Sheol" (2:2 ESV): "Sheol" is the closest Old Testament term to "hell." Yet from within "the belly of Sheol," Jonah declares, "Salvation belongs to the LORD!" (2:9).

This undermines the Cynic's arrogant claim to have discovered everything. The Cynic believes that having gotten to the bottom of the political world's stories, he has discovered the whole truth: there is only pain and ugliness. God invites the Cynic to grow in humility, not by somehow brainwashing the Cynic to forget what he has discovered, but by revealing what the Cynic has missed up to now: that within all of that discovered pain and ugliness, God is still present to save people.

Another term for this kind of humility-inducing process is *awe*. Awe occurs when someone senses there is something profoundly more—more powerful, more beautiful, more meaningful—than he can fully know. This is why awe leads to humility. Spiritual awe occurs when someone realizes that this more is God himself and recognizes that God's presence is far deeper than what our knowledge can fully capture. Interestingly, researchers have discovered that the experience of awe is one of the most effective interventions in politically polarized conflicts, as "awe leads to increased humility, a diminished sense of self, an increased awareness of how one is embedded in social networks, and an awareness of shared humanity with others."[1]

We tend to experience awe when we lift our eyes upward to a beautiful scene, like the vast canopy of stars, blinking millions of light-years away. But in the realm of politics, we more often experience awe when we dig into our painful experiences and discover that God is still present with us in the depths. Sean and Emily Harris experienced awe in the midst of their conflict with Sean's parents. Nancy and Kathy experienced awe after being mired in online conflict. For all of them, their experience in the depths resulted in humility.

Chapter 2 of Jonah is a poetic break in the larger story; it is meant to give the reader a window into this kind of humility-inducing awe before resuming the narrative. Let's take this break now ourselves.

---

1. Andy Tix, "Awe Experiences Decrease Political Polarization," *Psychology Today*, February 22, 2021, www.psychologytoday.com/us/blog/the-pursuit-peace/202102/awe-experiences-decrease-political-polarization.

REFLECTION EXERCISE

1. Still your mind for a minute and invite the Holy Spirit to show you God's truth for you.

2. Then read Jonah 2 slowly and prayerfully.

3. Next ask God to bring to mind a life experience that resonates with Jonah's experience in the belly of Sheol. It could be an experience related to politics, and if something comes up in that realm, go with it. But God may also prompt an experience from another realm of your life: health, relationships, career, or something else. That's fine—go with whatever God prompts.

    As you reflect on that experience through the lens of Jonah 2, try to remember how God's presence showed up within that painful or ugly experience. What form did his presence take? What did it feel like to fall into God's presence at that time?

4. Hold on to that feeling, and now try to apply that feeling to how you feel about politics. Contemplate the possibility that God may somehow still be

present in all that you find painful and ugly about politics. How close can you come to imagining that possibility? Don't put any pressure on yourself to feel anything inauthentic, but do open yourself up to God's prompting. What might change for you if you could come closer to experiencing God's saving presence within the ugliness and pain of politics?

GOD'S HOPE FOR THE NATIONS

Having been rescued by the Lord in the depths, Jonah is now filled with awe and humility. This is a critical transformation for the Cynic. After the fish spits him out onto a beach, and Jonah shakes off the slime and gunk, he expresses this transformation via a newfound resolve to obey the original command to go to Nineveh. He arrives at Nineveh, and there at the center of the capital he "called out, 'Yet forty days, and Nineveh shall be overthrown!'" (Jonah 3:4 ESV).

What happens next is a political miracle, as awesome and humility inducing in its own way as a divine intervention via a giant fish. The text describes the response: "And the people of Nineveh believed God. They called for a fast and put on sackcloth, from the greatest of them to the least of them" (v. 5 ESV).

The odds of this happening were incredibly remote. No

political pundit—had they existed in the ancient Near East—would have predicted this outcome. An entire nation is led toward change, not by the external force of coercive power (such as a foreign invasion), but by the purely spiritual and non-violent appeal of a prophet. Jonah didn't even hope for this miraculous response from his political enemies. Jonah probably hoped the Lord would miraculously rescue him from the violent political backlash, akin to the way he was rescued from drowning. As is revealed later in the story, Jonah didn't think his listeners would actually repent.

It is important to reflect on God's saving power on the small scale of our individual lives, like we did in the reflection exercise. But it is also important to be open to the possibility of large-scale political miracles. They have occurred in our own modern era. Earlier in the book, we mentioned the miracle that was the modern civil rights movement. If you teleported back to the early 1950s before the advent of this movement, no major political pundit would have predicted the end of Jim Crow segregation in the South and the implementation of robust anti-discrimination policies in the north. Our country was mired in the depths of racial injustice. But twenty years later, this transformation was underway. Yes, this national transformation was incomplete then and is still today marked by human fallibility and hypocrisy. But an unexpected and miraculous transformation undoubtedly occurred.

In this national miracle, God called his prophets—followers

of Jesus like Dr. Martin Luther King Jr. and Rosa Parks—to confront the nation with the biblical message of justice. Plus, our leaders—men like president Lyndon B. Johnson—overcame their own cultural backgrounds and admitted the need for national repentance, causing them to sign landmark legislation like the 1965 Civil Rights Act, which (among other accomplishments) named racially based violence as a federal crime. Such an act is analogous to the king of Assyria issuing a ruling that called the entire nation to repentance, when he confessed the violent nature of his own culture: "Let everyone turn from his evil way and from the violence that is in his hands" (Jonah 3:8 ESV).

Modern American civil rights legislation and the king of Assyria's proclamation both focused on violence as the national sin. In the stories of America and Assyria, God's ultimate intention is to heal the national impulse toward violence. This is why, once the king of Assyria repented of violence and aligned himself and his nation with God's intention, God quickly "relented of the disaster that he had said he would do to them, and he did not do it" (3:10 ESV).

The healing of political violence is God's ultimate hope for every nation in every era. The Bible makes this intention clear in its various descriptions of that future day when God will finally fulfill his hope for all nations. One of the most beautiful descriptions of that final future that the Scriptures call "the latter days" is found in the words of another of Israel's prophets, Isaiah. Isaiah 2:1–5 is a classic example of the vision of these "latter days," and it includes this promise:

> And they shall beat their swords into plowshares,
>   and their spears into pruning hooks;
> nation shall not lift up sword against nation,
>   neither shall they learn war anymore.
>
> **—ISAIAH 2:4 ESV**

"Nations" in the biblical sense should be understood as tribes and not just formally constituted countries. This biblical vision of the latter days includes ending the conflict between warring political tribes within a modern nation-state like America.

In the latter days, God will end violence within and among nations. God revealed this hopeful vision in Jesus. Every gospel account is crystal clear that Jesus refrained from violence and absolutely commanded his followers to follow his model. For instance, when one of his disciples strikes at the arresting mob with a sword, Jesus replies in a command that echoes back to the imagery of Isaiah 2:4: "Put your sword back into its place. For all who take the sword will perish by the sword. Do you think that I cannot appeal to my Father, and he will at once send me more than twelve legions of angels? But how then should the Scriptures be fulfilled, that it must be so?" (Matt. 26:52–54 ESV).

As Jesus said in Matthew 26:54, the Scriptures (like the beautiful vision of Isaiah 2) are fulfilled in Jesus on the cross, where Jesus absorbed the full force of human fallibility, hypocrisy, conflict, and violence. He took all of it upon himself and extinguished it. Ephesians describes humanity as defined by warring camps and proclaims that Jesus reconciled "us both to God in one body through the cross, thereby killing the hostility. And he came and preached peace to you who were far off and peace to those who were near" (Eph. 2:16–17 ESV).

Political violence causes conflict, destruction, and death. The kingdom of God brings an end to all sources of conflict, destruction, and death. This is why Jesus refused to engage in political violence and commands his disciples to follow his model.

The enmity between red and blue continues to grow daily, and we now face a growing number of false Christian teachers spewing the heresy that followers of Jesus should take up arms as happened at the insurrection on January 6, 2021. That date is an unmistakable sign: the threat of political violence is real. Conflict, destruction, and death have already occurred.

Yet as dire as our current situation seems, God is at work to end violence and bring the world closer to that final day when all peoples shall beat their swords into plowshares and their spears into pruning hooks.

God advances his work through his people. He worked through prophets like Jonah and Dr. Martin Luther King Jr. He worked through rulers like the king of Assyria and Lyndon B.

Johnson. But he also worked through the everyday people of every era. He worked through the many residents of Nineveh that believed, fasted, put on sackcloth, and repented. He worked through the multitudes of Americans of every color that marched, spoke, and voted their way toward a vision of racial justice and peace. And in our moment, he will work through the millions of Christians who still recognize that following Jesus requires putting away the sword and embracing God's eternal hope to end conflict, death, and destruction among the nations.

If you are reading this book, this is a sign that God seeks to work through you. God invites you to share in his hopes for your little corner of the nation. In your neighborhood, school, church, or family, you have an assigned role. You may be the reluctant messenger like Jonah, the person with some power like the king of Assyria, a member of the wider audience like Nineveh's residents, or some other role. Whatever it is, you have been assigned a part to play in God's big story.

To inhabit our role, God is inviting every one of his actors to plumb the depths. Not to the depths of ideology, party, or policies—we should already know that we will find at the bottom of that kind of story plenty of human fallibility, hypocrisy, and sin. No, we have to dig into the depths of our own hearts, and examine whether we truly share in God's hope for our nation and all nations. Do we share in God's eternal hope to end conflict, death, and destruction?

This is not a simple question with an obvious answer. But it is a question that takes us deeper into God's hope for the nations—and for each one of us.

THE DEPTHS OF OUR HEARTS

As we enter the fourth and final chapter of the book of Jonah, we see that the prophet has come a long way. As a Cynic, he began with low hope and low humility. His humility has risen through spiritual awe; he has experienced God's saving power for himself in the depths.

But when he sees that the Assyrians actually repent and are welcomed by God, Jonah reveals what lies in the depths of his own heart. The reader might expect that the Assyrian response would have led to Jonah's joy. But read carefully Jonah's response: "But it displeased Jonah exceedingly, and he was angry. And he prayed to the LORD and said, 'O LORD, is not this what I said when I was yet in my country? That is why I made haste to flee to Tarshish; for I knew that you are a gracious God and merciful, slow to anger and abounding in steadfast love, and relenting from disaster. Therefore now, O LORD, please take my life from me, for it is better for me to die than to live'" (Jonah 4:1–3 ESV).

Why is Jonah "exceedingly displeased" and "angry"? Because Jonah is now finally confronted with the remaining layer of the Cynic's heart: he does not share in God's hope for the nations. He reveals that he did not want to serve as a vehicle for God's mercy. He knew God's merciful character and did not want the Assyrians to benefit from "a gracious God . . . slow to anger and abounding in steadfast love, and relenting from disaster."

Why this resistance? The us-versus-them mindset had become buried deeply in Jonah's psyche. Perhaps the Assyrians had already killed his friends and family, and he harbors grievances and bitterness. Perhaps he finds the Assyrian culture deeply repulsive and so "other" that he cannot stand the idea of being joined to them in God's mercy. Perhaps Jonah also thinks the Assyrian show of repentance is superficial and cannot be genuine. People and institutions cannot change that fast, can they? The Cynic would cross his arms and raise an eyebrow at that kind of hope. The Cynic would be displeased at having to uncross his arms to embrace his enemies. *Please. Let's not be so naive.*

Whatever Jonah's reason, many can relate to his resistance, whether we are Cynics, Combatants, Exhausted, or Disciples. Think about the most hated public figure that represents the *them* in your own political spectrum. Imagine God extending grace and mercy toward that figure. Imagine God extending himself toward that hated figure *before* this person repents. Note that God was offering himself to the Assyrians in the form of sending Jonah even before they repented. Their repentance allowed them to experience God's mercy from their end, but the Lord was already reaching out to them from his end while they were still in their evil state. Can you imagine the Lord doing that with your political enemies?

Now imagine yourself as Jonah. Like Jonah, you stand before God looking at your enemy. And God is telling you that, in his eyes, you and your enemy are far more similar than different. What feelings arise? Does that help you empathize with the displeasure and anger that arose in Jonah?

What do we do with our own versions of displeasure and anger? What do we do with our own revulsion at the idea that our political enemies are also children of God—and thus that we belong to the same family?

We urgently need God to get to the depths of our own hearts, to that place where resistance and revulsion reside. If we do not believe that God can ultimately save enemies, what hope is there for us? We were once enemies of God (Rom. 5:10–21; Col. 1:21–22). Our hope for our own salvation rests on God's love for those that oppose him, because all of us have harbored enmity toward God.

Similarly, if we do not believe that God can reunite *us* with *them*, what hope do we have for our world that is so consumed by such division? If God's reconciliation is a pipe dream, then we are all consigned to a world of interminable conflict. We all teeter ever closer to despair where we would echo Jonah's plaintive plea: "Therefore now, O Lord, please take my life from me, for it is better for me to die than to live" (Jonah 4:3 ESV).

In the story, the Lord recognizes the spiritual danger of despair that threatens his prophet. The Lord asks Jonah to reflect more deeply on his peril: "And the LORD said, 'Do you do well to be angry?'" (v. 4 ESV).

Jonah ignores this question. Instead, he physically enacts the spiritual posture of the Cynic: "Jonah went out of the city and sat to the east of the city and made a booth for himself there. He sat under it in the shade, till he should see what would become of the city" (v. 5 ESV). He sits back in judgmental disengagement. If growing in God's hope for the world means embracing those he finds deplorable, he will sit it out.

This is now the second time that Jonah has rejected God's invitation. Yet God will not give up on trying to reach his Cynic. God's next move is to create a plant to give Jonah shade, "to save him from his discomfort" (v. 6 ESV). Jonah deeply appreciates this act of divine mercy, but then God "appointed a worm that attacked the plant, so that it withered" (v. 7 ESV). God allows "a scorching east wind" and hot sun to come upon Nineveh (v. 8 ESV). This is most likely what modern meteorologists call a sirocco, a rare but particularly devastating phenomenon; it was also known as "blood rain" because it stirred up masses of red dust that could choke out all who fell under it.

Standing outside the city, Jonah suffers along with all the residents. He teeters further into despair and repeats his plaintive cry to God, "I'm so angry I wish I were dead" (v. 9). Pay

close attention to the ensuing dialogue between God and Jonah
(vv. 9–11 ESV):

> **God:** Do you do well to be angry for the plant?
> **Jonah:** Yes, I do well to be angry, angry enough to die.
> **God:** You pity the plant, for which you did not labor,
> nor did you make it grow, which came into being
> in a night and perished in a night. And should not
> I pity Nineveh, that great city, in which there are
> more than 120,000 persons who do not know their
> right hand from their left, and also much cattle?

God patiently invites Jonah back into his story of redemptive hope, which encompasses all of humanity. The plant evokes the Eden story and its fundamental truth: all humans—of every political tribe—are created in the image of God and meant to dwell together in the garden, tending to and benefiting from creation. The dying plant represents the effect of human sin that brought division, death, and destruction into this world. But the story of humanity is not meant to remain stuck there. God in his infinite grace and mercy has pity on all of humanity. God seeks to end the division, death, and destruction. He has signified his intention with the Assyrians' repentance, and he will achieve peace decisively and fully for all nations in "the latter days" described in Isaiah 2.

God now invites Jonah to fulfill his assigned role with all of his heart, including that last layer that holds out against God's pity for his political opponents. God seeks to engage Jonah's sympathy for the people of Nineveh by pointing out that their behavior, while certainly infected with sin, is also the product of sheer lack of knowledge: they are people "who do not know their right hand from their left." Further reinforcing God's invitation to sympathy is the fact that Jonah and the Ninevites now suffer equally under the blood rain.

The book ends by leaving Jonah standing outside the city contemplating this invitation. The Bible doesn't tell us how he finally responds, which is a sure sign that God wants the question to be hanging around for future readers like us.

CURTIS'S STORY

I experienced my version of Jonah's dialogue with God in late 2020. At that time, I had just begun to cautiously reengage the political world as a Christian. For many months, the entire world had been suffering from the COVID-19 pandemic that had left a swath of death and destruction. We were now hearing that relief from this crisis was on the horizon with the availability of vaccines.

I suspect that one reason God so patiently seeks out Cynics like Jonah and me to play a role in his story is that Cynics do have a particular gift to bring to the party: we see the problems with both sides. In my case, as a consultant to secular nonprofits, I knew the heads of local public-health agencies that were going to be tasked with the public information campaign promoting the vaccine. Almost all of them were progressives, and they were receiving funding from federal programs designed by a liberal administration. In my conversations with them, I discovered—to no great surprise—that practically all the campaigns were designed with a racial-identity lens: the outreach was exclusively targeted at communities of color. There was no program designed to reach White conservative evangelicals, which data was already showing to be the largest vaccine-hesitant population. Secular public health—with its typically progressive blind spots—was completely ignoring the most important target population. The left hand, so to speak, was not even thinking about the right hand.

At the same time, conservative White evangelicals were being swamped with misinformation since the initial response to the pandemic had been politicized. Conservative White distrust of public-health institutions was riding high, and the vaccine was being swept up in that wave of misinformation and distrust. The right hand was primed to reject anything proffered by the left hand.

Over the next year, I led my team at Redeeming Babel (the nonprofit that is behind *The After Party* project) to create the Christians and the Vaccine campaign. We tried to put ourselves in the mindset of conservative evangelicals and address respectfully their fears about the vaccine, including tackling topics such as "Can you be pro-life and pro-vaccine?" "Is the vaccine a form of governmental control?" and, the one that was the most popular, "Is the vaccine the 'mark of the beast'?" Our campaign became the leading national effort to persuade vaccine-hesitant evangelicals. And I was given the opportunity to testify before the US Senate on the urgent need for secular public health to approach religious conservatives with greater humility, respect, and investment.

In the process, I was reminded of some painful realities in the world of politics. The tendency for progressive elites to ignore—and often disdain—religious conservatives is real and ugly. I had to work with officials who looked at me with incredulity when I explained that Christians read passages such as Revelation 13:16–17 (about the mark of the beast) as the words of God—and I was one of those Christians.

At the same time, I had to deal with racist online commentary that evoked my childhood memories of those "Ching Chong Chang" taunts. The presence of racism within conservative politics is just as real, and it's ugly. I had to ask myself, "Do I really want to try to save the lives of people who seem to hate my people?"

There's no question that painful and ugly realities exist in politics. The question is whether I believe those realities are all that is there. If so, then I'm like Jonah, sitting outside the city and outside the hope of God. But the true "sign of Jonah" (Matt. 16:4) is an invitation to look more deeply and discover that God is there in the depths, extending his mercy to all. I experienced the privilege of serving as a small conduit of God's mercy to both progressive health officials and conservative evangelicals. God is the same God rescuing both sides.

Throughout the campaign, I encountered many little signs pointing the way out of cynicism and despair. I heard stories (and also received correlating data)[2] of people changing their own minds or using the videos to reopen conversations with vaccine-hesitant family and friends. I don't know how many lives were touched, but I'm looking forward to meeting those people in the latter days predicted by Isaiah. Imagining that future event fills me with hope.

I don't want to be left out of that day. So I'm no longer sitting out today as a Cynic. I'm moving toward the Disciple, one step at a time.

---

2. James Chu, Sophia L. Pink, and Robb Willer, "Religious Identity Cues Increase Vaccination Intentions and Trust in Medical Experts among American Christians," *PNAS* 118, no. 49 (2021), www.pnas.org/doi/10.1073/pnas.2106481118.

REFLECTION EXERCISE

1. What are some local problems in your neighborhood or locality that affect everyone, regardless of their positions on national politics?

2. Which of these problems tug at your heart?

3. What are some opportunities to work on these local problems alongside others (including those who may hold different political views)?

4. Ask God if he might be inviting you to explore getting involved.

CHAPTER 6

THE TRUE
AFTER PARTY

CURTIS'S STORY

Do you have a recurring nightmare where you are failing a test?

I suffer from two versions of this nightmare. One takes me back to high school where, in my dream, I go through a series of anxious realizations. The dream begins in the morning when I wake up with the sudden awareness that there is a final exam that day in math class. I then recognize I have been skipping that class regularly and am grossly unprepared. I have a bright idea: I'll phone in with a fake excuse of being sick! That will give me more time to study! That's when I come to the final pit-in-the-stomach realization: I've pulled that trick for every previous math test that semester, and I have yet to make up a single one of them. I'll never catch up. It is hopeless.

My other version takes me back in a dream to senior year in college. I have one final exam to pass in order to graduate. I show up on campus but suddenly realize that I do not know where the exam is being held. I furiously run through buildings looking for the right place, but I cannot find it. These nightmares never end in any resolution. I have to keep running from one place to another, and I usually awake from this nightmare gasping for air. If humility is being content to admit "I don't know all the answers," then this is a nightmare mocking humility: I don't even know where I'm supposed to submit the answers, but I cannot rest in that unresolved state.

It is remarkable how many people suffer from some version of the test nightmare. One survey revealed that it is one of the most common recurring nightmares, afflicting over one-third of respondents.[1] Many of us seem to have a visceral fear of failing tests.

The politics of us versus them preys on this visceral

---

1. Andrea Chipman, "What Does It Mean When You Dream You Haven't Studied for a Big Test?" *Newsweek*, June 21, 2022, www.newsweek.com/dream-about-being-unprepared-exam-not-studied-test-recurring-dreams-explained-1717439.

fear. People must be tested and sorted accordingly: Are you with us? Are you with them? The subject matter of those tests is not a feared high school subject (like math, for me) but the latest issue in the *what* story of politics that features ideology, party, and policy.

I encounter these tests everywhere, coming from both sides. In my church, a Black member of the pastoral staff wears a Black Lives Matter shirt every time she appears on the worship stage. Whatever her intent, her choice of apparel effectively has functioned as a recurrent test of ideology for members. Our progressive members applaud this act as a protest against racial inequality, while conservative members complain about the national BLM organization's ideological affinity with Marxism. In my Bay Area neighborhood, one house has stood out in recent election seasons by boldly displaying pro-Trump signs and banners. Cars will slow down in front of this house and lower windows, with most occupants expressing incredulity and disgust. A few honk and raise their fist in solidarity. It seems like anything—clothing, yard signs, bumper stickers, favorite musicians, and more—can get coded into a political test for everyone to take.

Like our nightmares, political tests can be utterly irrational. Take the policy of vaccination that we addressed in the Christians and the Vaccine campaign.

Before the pandemic, White evangelical Christians historically supported the policy of mandatory vaccination in overwhelming numbers.[2] But as soon as COVID-19 responses got tagged with political colors, White evangelicals flipped entirely on this policy issue. Showing your partisan loyalty became more urgent than protecting the health of one's family and community.

To repeat, both sides will look for indicators—small tests of loyalty—that reduce everything to the question of "Are you with us? Or are you with them?" In the vaccine campaign, a tense moment occurred for me with the most politically Left-leaning member of my consulting firm, a woman I've worked with for years. She is not a Christian, did not know about my evangelical religious identity, and hadn't been tracking my side efforts around the vaccine. Since I was about to testify before the US Senate, I needed to tell her that I was leading this effort to reach evangelicals before she heard about it secondhand.

When I called her up and explained what I was doing and why, there was a long silent beat on the other end. I tried to break the awkward gap: "So, do you have any questions about any of this?"

2. Adelle M. Banks, "More Evangelicals Oppose School Vaccine Requirements," *Christianity Today*, May 17, 2023, www.christianitytoday.com/news/2023/may/vaccines-risks-schools-evangelical-children-survey.html.

More silence.

Finally she said incredulously, "You're an evangelical?"

Her response indicates how the evangelical religious identity has become coded in the public eye with Right-wing *what* politics. This coding is why for years—especially as a Cynic trying to sit it out—I operated in my liberal Bay Area nonprofit sector as a "closet evangelical." If I somehow got outed (anyone googling me can discover that I used to serve as a senior pastor of an Evangelical Covenant Church), I would embark on long, awkward disclaimers along the lines of "Um, I'm not *that* kind of evangelical." But in this conversation, I decided to reclaim the theological definition of *evangelical*—which has far deeper historic roots than the recent political highjacking of the term. I simply said, "Yes, I'm an evangelical in my religious beliefs."

She was quiet for another long time, then finally stammered, "I'm just trying to get my head around this. You're kind of messing with my mind. But the work we've done together . . . you've always been so inclusive, progressive, and rational. So, wait, you're an evangelical?"

I could practically hear her mental gears straining. *Wait, I thought you belonged to us. Are you actually one of them?*

This book has been demonstrating that following Jesus means leaving behind the us-versus-them mindset. But you won't get to graduate without exams. The world will inevitably subject you to political loyalty tests.

We need Jesus to teach us how to face such tests. Left to our own devices, our fear of failing these tests will paralyze us in our ongoing growth toward hope and humility. It's hard to feel hopeful when you sense that you're failing in the eyes of others; it's difficult to rest in humility when others are demanding that you supply the right answer.

We are nearing the conclusion of *The After Party*. It is time to learn from our Master Teacher on how to prepare for the final exam.

FROM TESTS TO SIGNS

Jesus faced the same kind of political test. Matthew 16:1 describes one example: "And the Pharisees and Sadducees came, *and to test him* they asked him to show them a sign from heaven" (ESV, emphasis mine). Pharisees and Sadducees were bitterly opposed on the big political issues of the day, but they agreed that it was most important to pin Jesus down.

The fact that these two bitter enemies joined together to test Jesus reveals how much Jesus frustrated and confused both of their sides.

The two sides especially wanted to force Jesus to do a

miracle—"a sign from heaven"—that would reveal his political colors. His previous miracles had been too politically ambiguous for them. For instance, immediately before this test in Matthew 16, Jesus accomplished the miracle of feeding the four thousand (Matt. 15:32–38). But what did this miracle signify politically? In first-century politics, a prophetic leader feeding the masses like that was often a key strategy in mobilizing a mass rebellion.[3] Feed the hungry—the poor who would have been the most disaffected with the ruling regime—and you've got yourself a potential rebel army. He even accomplishes the miracle with suggestive signs of military organization, such as deliberately ordering the masses into smaller units commanded by his subordinates (vv. 35–36). Many Zealots and some Pharisees would eagerly welcome such a sign as the beginnings of an ultranationalist Jewish rebellion, but the Sadducees and tax collectors would have grown anxious about such a threat to the status quo.

But then, just as quickly, Jesus dismissed the crowds and retreated by boat to an obscure region, as if to signify that he harbored no rebellious design (15:39). The act suggests that maybe he was just a harmless religious teacher of privatized truths, maybe a mystic of some sort. Now the Sadducees and tax collectors would have breathed a sigh of relief, and those opposing the current regime would have felt disappointed.

3. Oleg Kostyuk, "The Function of Military Language in the Feeding of the Five Thousand Narrative (Mark 6:30–44): A Narrative-Cognitive Study" (dissertation, Andrews University, 2020), https://digitalcommons.andrews.edu/cgi/viewcontent.cgi?article=3008&context=dissertations.

What is Jesus up to? *Are you with us? Or are you with them?* Jesus' refusal to conform to the binary options of the day drives the existing parties to distraction. Note that the Pharisees became so obsessed with forcing Jesus into an existing side that they made a similar move again later in Matthew 22. There they conspired with another opposing party—the Herodians—to try to trap Jesus into taking a policy position on Roman taxation (Matt. 22:15–22).

All the parties—the Pharisees, Sadducees, and Herodians—demand that Jesus take a side, any side. That on multiple occasions these political enemies will collude to force this test on Jesus reveals a truth about partisans across the ages: they can become so committed to the us-versus-them mindset that upholding the division itself becomes weirdly even more important than beating the other side. *Us* hates *them*, but both sides together hate even more someone who refuses to play by their rules.

Jesus refuses. He refuses to allow his politics to be forcibly reduced into their either-or categories. He refuses to take their tests. Pay careful attention to how Jesus responds in Matthew 16: "He answered them, 'When it is evening, you say, "It will be fair weather, for the sky is red." And in the morning, "It will be stormy today, for the sky is red and threatening." You know how to interpret the appearance of the sky, but you cannot interpret the signs of the times. An evil and adulterous generation seeks for a sign, but no sign will be given to it except the sign of Jonah.' So he left them and departed" (vv. 2–4 ESV).

In the Gospels, when Jesus faces a false test that presents only wrong options, he usually responds with a parable or analogy to reframe the topic and illuminate the deeper error. Here, Jesus responds to the demand for a test with his comments about weather signs. What does this analogy mean?

Jesus is reframing politics by shifting the emphasis from tests to signs. The Pharisees and the Sadducees—this "evil and adulterous generation"—approach Jesus under the guise of looking for a sign, but as verse 1 has already made clear, their actual intent is to test him. What is the key difference between a test and a sign? A test frames current events as declarations of current loyalties. A sign frames current events as pointers to a future event.

Jesus is telling his inquisitors, "If you were genuinely looking for a sign from me, you wouldn't be testing me to fit me into your existing partisan options; instead, you would be seeking me in order to understand the future." Weather signs are meant to direct us toward a future event, not to lock us into present-day sides. We look at the "red sky" not to prove our loyalty to the color red but because it points to the stormy day to come. Everyone else—the Pharisees and Sadducees of yesterday, the red and blue of today—view the political climate as filled with color-coded tests of current party loyalty. Jesus points to what happens *after* those party colors fade from the sky.

If you wish to adopt the better politics of Jesus, the key is to grasp his *after*, his vision of the future. Throughout the Gospels,

Jesus has been hinting at a future decisive event that centers around him. For a Disciple, this future event of Jesus unlocks the true meaning of current events. Adopting this perspective is what it means to correctly interpret the signs of the times. We must first grasp this final event centered on Jesus; then and only then can we properly work backward from that future event to recognize how current events can serve as signposts.

What, then, is this big future event of Jesus?

THE AFTER PARTY OF JESUS

The Pharisees and Sadducees are not genuinely seeking to be taught by Jesus, but even to this "evil and adulterous generation" Jesus offers a breadcrumb trail to his future. It's a sign that readers should recognize from the previous chapter. Jesus offers them "the sign of Jonah" (Matt. 16:4 ESV).

We learned in the previous chapter that the "sign of Jonah" points to God's future when the Lord finally brings an end to conflict and violence. Recall the king of Assyria's original response to Jonah, when he called to the Ninevites: "Let *everyone* turn from his evil way and from the violence that is in his hands" (Jonah 3:8 ESV, emphasis added). In Jesus, God is now extending that call to everyone, including the Pharisees and Sadducees standing before him in Matthew 16. Jesus already had explained this interpretation of the sign of Jonah a few passages earlier in Matthew 12 when he proclaimed, "The

men of Nineveh will rise up at the judgment with this generation and condemn it, for they repented at the preaching of
Jonah, and behold, something greater than Jonah is here" (v. 41
ESV). The original sign of Jonah was a preview of Jesus. Jesus
now stands as the fulfillment of that preview; he is the ultimate
sign of Jonah that conveys God's universal invitation to a final
and lasting peace.

How will God achieve this final peace? The decisive event
will be the cross. How Jesus will die is also part of the sign of
Jonah. As Jesus explains, "For just as Jonah was three days and
three nights in the belly of the great fish, so will the Son of
Man be three days and three nights in the heart of the earth"
(Matt. 12:40 ESV). In his death and resurrection, Jesus will
absorb the full force of the political world's impulses of conflict
and violence. It is important to note that as evangelicals we
have been so overly conditioned to focus on individual salvation—as important and necessary as that is—that we tend to
miss the political implications of the cross. Roman crucifixion
was reserved for political crimes alone. And the gospel narra-
tives consistently narrate the crucifixion to show that it was
not one individual or personal act that crucified Jesus. The
type of human sin that most directly crucified Jesus is best
categorized as political sin: the collusion of the fallen politics
of the Pharisees, Sadducees, Herodians, Zealots (it was most
likely two Zealot bandits who hung on either side of Jesus),
and the Roman Empire (as embodied in the craven ruling of

Pilate). If Jesus was only teaching about the spiritual life of privatized individuals—as important as that topic is—the crucifixion simply would not have happened. Strip Jesus of his agenda for a radical new peace under his authority—an agenda that threatened the prevailing rules of politics and unsettled all the parties—and the entire gospel narrative doesn't quite make sense.

We thus have to understand the cross as the decisive event when Jesus absorbs all of the world's political and spiritual enmity into himself. By doing this, by suffering it in his body, Jesus transforms enmity into God's mercy, forgiveness, and ultimate peace. It is as if on the cross his body digests the human virus of endemic conflict, and his blood possesses the spiritual antibodies to transform the virus into a vaccine. In his resurrection, he proves that his spiritual vaccine works: his blood can triumph over the worst that conflict can inflict, which is death itself.

This political interpretation of Jesus' death and resurrection is congruent with the more pervasive interpretation that concentrates on personal and individual salvation. Passages like Ephesians 2:13–16 describe this congruence: "But now in Christ Jesus you who once were far off have been brought near by the blood of Christ. For he himself is our peace, who has made us both one and has broken down in his flesh the dividing wall of hostility by abolishing the law of commandments expressed in ordinances, that he might create in himself one new man in place of the two, so making peace, and might reconcile us both to God in one body through the cross, thereby killing the hostility" (ESV).

Note how the blood overcomes the division between you and God *and* the division between us and them. One leads to the other. The crucifixion of Jesus "has broken down in his flesh the dividing wall of hostility" such that personal reconciliation with God leads to sociopolitical reconciliation with others. In the blood of Christ, we become one blood. In the body of Christ, we become one body.

As Ephesians 2 references, the early church initially focused this peacemaking power on the us-versus-them division most immediately threatening its own community: the sociopolitical division between Jew and Gentile. But God always meant for the peace accomplished in the cross to keep extending outward to every other us-versus-them conflict in the world, so that among the people of God, "there is not Greek and Jew, circumcised and uncircumcised, barbarian, Scythian, slave, free; but Christ is all, and in all" (Col. 3:11 ESV).

The peace of the cross is meant to keep rippling out, as sign after sign pointing to God's final future, which the Old Testament calls the "latter days." This is when the Lord returns to earth and all the nations will learn from the Lord to "beat their swords into plowshares, and their spears into pruning hooks; nation shall not lift up sword against nation, neither shall they learn war anymore" (Isa. 2:4 ESV).

This final fulfillment will be a glorious and festive day. Isaiah elsewhere describes it as a grand feast:

> On this mountain the LORD of hosts will make
>> for all peoples
>> a feast of rich food, a feast of well-
>> aged wine,
>> of rich food full of marrow, of aged wine
>> well refined.
> And he will swallow up on this mountain
>> the covering that is cast over all peoples,
>> the veil that is spread over all nations.

—ISAIAH 25:6–7 ESV

This final achievement of peace "over all nations" is indeed marked by a party. This is why the final book of the Bible describes this final event as the "wedding supper of the Lamb" (Rev. 19:9). It's a perfect metaphor. The paradigmatic act of a wedding is the union of those who have previously lived apart. The feast expresses the joy that this union sparks. The Lamb marks how Jesus accomplished this union by absorbing all conflict onto himself and transforming it into peace. This peace will prevail between us and God *and* between us and them; there is no longer any us versus them but rather only one *us* fully reunited with one God.

That final and future event will be a glorious celebration of the peacemaking victory of Jesus. All the political parties today, with all their conflict and division, will be transformed into a final party. All the partisan colors will fade from the sky and give way to the glorious after party of Jesus.

When will this after party happen? Jesus tells his disciples that no one knows the "day or hour" (Mark 13:32). We are not supposed to correlate current events with the precise timing of the after party of Jesus. Rather, we are called to correlate current events with the true character of the after party. That's what a sign does: it helps you anticipate how things will be when you arrive at your final destination. A highway sign displaying the icon of a bed anticipates a hotel; the icons of food tell you a restaurant awaits you. Like Jesus did in Matthew 16, the creative task of the Disciple is to convert political litmus tests into signs. Like Jesus, we respond to today's partisan pressures by creating living icons pointing to the after party.

For the Disciple, this is going to require a great deal of relearning and creativity, because this is not the way the world trains us to approach politics. The secular political industry and media will keep pulling us into the divisions of ideology, party, and policy. Unfortunately, too many of our religious teachers are themselves like the Pharisees and Sadducees when it comes to reducing politics to a series of tests discovering whether, as Christians, you are *us* or *them*. We need to be especially vigilant in guarding our minds against ostensibly Christian teaching that draws us back into that partisan mindset. This is why, after giving the sign of Jonah, Jesus privately warns his disciples, "Watch and beware of the leaven of the Pharisees and Sadducees" (Matt. 16:6 ESV). That the threat is the leaven of *both* sides makes it clear that the real danger for disciples is not holding the wrong policy positions but adopting the underlying us–versus–them mentality.

In that warning, Jesus is referencing the Jewish practice of cleaning yeast out of their homes to prepare for the Passover Feast of Unleavened Bread. In similar fashion, we need to clean out the us–versus–them mentality from our imaginations and prepare ourselves with signs of the feast that is the after party of Jesus.

CURTIS'S STORY

I have one such sign indelibly imprinted in my memory. I share it as an example of how disciples of Jesus can convert incredibly painful tests into profoundly hopeful signs.

My story takes place in 1992 in Soweto, South Africa. If you think current-day America seems hopelessly divided, well, as the old saying goes, "You ain't seen nothin' yet." At that time, South Africa was still defined by apartheid, the formal system that divided Blacks and Whites in practically every sphere of life. Nelson Mandela had just been released from prison, and his political party, the African National Congress, was locked in tense negotiations with the White Afrikaner government over the political future of the country.

I had just graduated from college and was still trying to figure out how my faith, race, and politics all fit together. This particular collision of identities defined South Africa, and I thought that living in that context might help me. I got connected to one of the few truly interracial churches in South Africa, a small church called Johweto. The name stood for the union of White Johannesburg and Black Soweto, hence Johweto. Even among the few interracial churches of the country, Johweto stood out as the only one (that I heard of) where the Whites actually traveled into the Black township to worship together. Under apartheid, this act was technically illegal. I joined the pastoral team of Johweto and chose to live in Soweto with Trevor, the young Black co-pastor of the church (who partnered with a White co-pastor). Trevor couldn't drive, so most of my pastoral work that year was driving him around Soweto in a beat-up Honda supplied by the church.

I was one of only a tiny handful of non-Blacks ever to have lived in Soweto up to that point in the country's history. I was violating both apartheid laws and the lived experience of Sowetans. For the first months, everywhere I walked crowds of young Black kids crowded around me as a curiosity, some of them making kung fu moves (apparently Bruce Lee movies had made it into the country). Eventually, the residents got used to me, and I was adopted as an honorary Black Sowetan. I was invited into the informal dinner parties and dances that composed the social scene of the township.

At the same time, because I was an American, White South Africans also welcomed me as an honorary "White" and invited me to their tea parties. Socially, I was like a ghost who could walk through the "dividing wall of hostility" in that country and hear how each side candidly felt about the other. It was fascinating and frightening. Even within Johweto, the two sides were so divided that I could not imagine how a postapartheid South Africa could exist.

Ironically, a White friend of mine from college also chose to work in South Africa that year. She got a job as a staff person for the high-level political negotiations between Mandela's African National Congress and the White government. We would see each other at political events and trade notes. I always felt insecure in those conversations. She was spending her year at the center of political history, and I was a glorified taxi driver.

On June 17 of that year, I was driving Trevor when we heard news of a large-scale massacre committed by masked gunmen in a nearby Black township of Boipatong. Throughout the year, there had been frequent acts of violence, but this took place on a larger scale, taking the lives of dozens of Black residents. The question of who was responsible became the dominant question of the day. What you thought had happened at Boipatong became the definitive political test. With my ghostlike status, I heard both sides become angrier and more insistent. In Black Sowetan dinner parties, I heard Blacks argue that of course the culprit was conservative White security forces. At White Johannesburg tea parties, I heard Whites label the massacre as Black-on-Black violence and further evidence of why Blacks could not be trusted to govern the country.

In ensuing weeks, the country teetered on the verge of splitting completely over this test and failing entirely. In our Sowetan home, I overheard Trevor field phone calls from fellow pastors inquiring if he knew how they could get their hands on an AK-47 automatic gun. White Johannesburg residents hired more armed security guards to guard their homes. Driving back from Johannesburg to Soweto in the day, I navigated my Honda between more and more government armored vehicles that were enforcing the boundary. At night in our home in Soweto, Trevor and I heard gunshots ring out with increasing frequency.

In late June, Mandela announced that he was pulling his party out of the negotiations, and all talks between the two sides collapsed. My friend was suddenly out of a job. Political commentators were predicting the advent of a racialized civil war. I wondered when I might have to get out of the country.

Johweto called an emergency prayer meeting on a Sunday evening. A handful of brave White members from Johannesburg drove to our house to join about a dozen equally brave Black members from Soweto. We were crowded in our living room, shoulder to shoulder. We then proceeded to do what Johweto termed "bleed over each other." Blacks gave expression to their rage and despair; Whites voiced their guilt and fear. We laid hands on each other in prayer; we sang worship songs that came to mind. We cried and moaned. We digested each other's pain.

As we bled over each other in this fashion, we felt a presence lifting us. The sensation was practically physical in nature, as we spontaneously got to our feet and started to dance in the township style of rhythmic stepping, where everyone circles up and locks arms, kicks and sways, hops and hangs on to each other for dear life. Someone started to laugh, and that laugh spread around the circle. It was nonsensical—this party breaking out amid the darkest of political crises—and yet it somehow made perfect sense.

I stood back for a moment to take in the scene. And inside me, I heard a voice say, *This is my body.*

PRACTICAL EXERCISE

For some, this calling to serve as a sign of the after party of Jesus may involve a project in your local community or church or perhaps joining some effort on a larger scale. But for everyone, this calling can most meaningfully take place in our individual relationships. Consider again your relationships lost or threatened by political division. How can you stand today as a humble sign of the final reconciliation of all things? How can you express your hope in the after party of Jesus?

The goal of this exercise is to create a sign within this relationship: an initial pointer away from political division back to the hope of a restored relationship. The exercise does this by guiding you both toward a conversation about how, even as you might hold politically opposing views, you might nevertheless share some things in common.

Here's the exercise:

- Identify someone from your disappeared ones list (see the exercise from the introduction) and ask for a conversation. This exercise might work best with someone who is also a follower of Jesus, but this is not required.

- Use the fact that you are reading this book (and/ or taking *The After Party* video course) as an excuse to reestablish contact. Explain how this book ends with this exercise. Ask if he or she would be willing to be your partner in this exercise.

- Explain to this person what you've learned about the distinction between *what* and *how*. To help the process, you can also ask this person to read the introduction and chapter 1 (feel free to share your copy of the book).

- Ask if he or she would be willing to take the Hope/Humility assessment and discuss the results with you (ideally in person).

- Agree together on the following ground rules of the conversation:
  - The conversation will follow the ten questions provided in the next section.
  - You two will not discuss or debate the *what* of politics. Differences in ideology, party, and policies are off-limits for this conversation. This is a conversation about what it is like to be a Combatant, Exhausted, Cynic, or Disciple.
  - Agree on a signal for when someone has crossed the line (for example, make a buzzer sound or do the time-out hand signal).
  - Each person will have one minute to answer each question. Use a timer and try to stick to the limit.
  - When each person speaks, the listener must not interrupt.
  - The only response allowed is an optional one: the listener can say, "That's interesting, tell me more." This will give the other person an additional (timed) minute to elaborate.

- Remember, the goal of this exercise is to see if talking about hope and humility can reopen the door with a disappeared one in your life. Neither of you is trying to change the other person's mind. It might be helpful to repeat (silently) to yourself these two words before and during the conversation with the other person: "Be curious."

Ten Questions

1. What profile (Combatant/Exhausted/Cynic/ Disciple) did the survey identify you as?

2. Do you believe this profile accurately depicts where you are in terms of politics? Why or why not?

3. Assuming there is at least some partial accuracy to the profile, how would you narrate why you currently identify with this profile?

4. Do you see this profile play out in other areas of your life besides politics? Can you illustrate?

5. Has your political life moved between the four quadrants in the past? If so, describe the trajectory.

6. Which profiles describe other people in your life? Elaborate.

7. How do you experience these other profiles? How do they make you feel?

8. How motivated are you to grow in hope and/or humility?

9. What is the strongest source of that motivation?

10. How did doing this exercise affect (if at all) how you think or feel?

CONCLUSION

The scene from Soweto described in the previous chapter depicts how the church turned a test into a sign. A political crisis that tested its unity was transformed into a preview of the after party of Jesus. Viewing it through the lens of hope and humility, we would like to believe that this transformation—and others like it—participated in the transformation of that entire divided country. While the peaceful transformation of apartheid South Africa into a multiracial democracy is not perfect, it is nevertheless a modern political miracle.

Such signs show that Jesus is present in his disciples in every political era, no matter how hopeless things seem. And because Jesus is present, we can be assured of our final future. Jesus will one day welcome us to the wedding feast of the Lamb, the joyful celebration of a deep and abiding peace over all conflicts afflicting all nations.

America is now facing its own version of such a test. On countless issues, we as a society are being forced into us versus them. From one election cycle to another, we wring our hands over whether our country will survive.

But we as Christians have been given the playbook for just such a moment. *The After Party* project takes place in a political context analogous to what Jesus faced in Matthew 16:1–6, when the Pharisees and the Sadducees conspired to subject him to their political test. Today's polarized politics similarly pressure American Christians to declare our allegiance to one party or another. Our project follows Jesus' model, one that refuses to conform to partisan tests of allegiance and instead creates signs of our highest allegiance to God's ultimate purpose.

As revealed in Jesus, God's ultimate purpose can be summed up in the word *reconciliation*. The early Christians constantly reminded themselves of this truth by repeating what scholars have called "the hymn of Christ" recorded in Colossians 1:15–20 (ESV): "He [Jesus] is the image of the invisible God, the firstborn of all creation. For by him all things were created, in heaven and on earth, visible and invisible, whether thrones or dominions or rulers or authorities—all things were created through him and for him. And he is before all things, and in him all things hold together. And he is the head of the body, the church. He is the beginning, the firstborn from the dead, that in everything he might be preeminent. For in him all the fullness of God was pleased to dwell, and through him to reconcile to himself all things, whether on earth or in heaven, making peace by the blood of his cross."

Note that the scope of this cosmic reconciliation includes the political realm. The terms "thrones or dominions or rulers or authorities" are explicitly taken from the political realm. Christians are to remind themselves that all politics ultimately belong to Jesus, for "all things were created through him and for him" (v. 16 ESV).

Therefore, this passage once again calls Christians to the spiritual values of humility and hope. All political allegiances must humble themselves before this highest loyalty, "that in everything he might be preeminent" (v. 18 ESV). And if we are tempted to hopelessness, filled with fear that today's political divisions will ultimately sever our relationships and our society, we are to remind ourselves that "in him all things hold together," and thus our ultimate future has already been secured in Jesus (v. 17 ESV). In Jesus, "all the fullness of God was pleased to dwell, and through him to reconcile to himself all things, whether on earth or in heaven, making peace by the blood of his cross" (vv. 19–20 ESV).

Christian politics is meant to stand as a humble sign pointing toward God's ultimate reconciliation of all things. A sign is intrinsically an expression of humility. A sign does not claim to capture all truths or convey the entire route; a sign needs only to point in the right direction wherever it is positioned. Therefore, you don't need to claim that you are correct on every specific political issue, much less follow all the ins and outs of politics. You just need to make sure that you are

pointing toward God's reconciliation wherever you are positioned, especially in your relationships. We hope this book has
given you some ideas about how to begin orienting yourselves
accordingly.

A sign is also an intrinsic expression of hope: it declares
that your desired destination indeed exists farther down the
road. Christian politics is meant to stand as a hopeful sign.
And Christians should be the most hopeful of people in politics. We're hopeful not because we think everything around
us will be fine—we are given no such promises. Nations rise
and nations fall. We should not allow the fiction of American
exceptionalism to make us think that the United States is
exempt from failure. And we certainly should not anchor our
hope on something as ephemeral as the next election results.

We are hopeful because everything is ultimately headed
toward God's final restoration of all things. We don't know the
convoluted path toward our final destination—and the journey
will certainly involve some painful bumps and bruises—but we
know we will arrive there in the end, made whole and fully
restored.

APPENDIX

Note: This is not a scientifically designed diagnostic quiz. These questions are meant to be lighthearted and are designed to be a bit exaggerated to prompt conversation.

Select the answers that most closely reflect your inclination when it comes to political topics and conversations.

ON HOPE

You're flipping through the channels on your TV or scrolling through social media and the latest political controversy appears. What do you do?

   a) Walk away from the TV or close the app. The news throws you into a state of despair about the world, and you'd rather ignore it.

   b) Leave the channel on or keep scrolling through the controversy for hours.

    c) Switch to another channel or app and look for something to distract you from all of the bad news.

    d) Take about thirty minutes to learn the details, then turn it off.

If someone were to ask whether you trust government leaders to make important decisions for the US, how would you reply?

    a) No. If they made it into office, then they're already corrupt.

    b) Not usually. They don't seem concerned with what's at stake in the decisions for people like me.

    c) Sometimes. I distrust some individuals but assume most are operating in good faith.

    d) Yes. The US Constitution establishes a framework and process for democratic participation and holding leadership accountable.

What do you do during an election year?

    a) Tune it all out. Conflict is uncomfortable, and in any case, you believe your vote doesn't really matter.

    b) Devote yourself to a platform or a party. You quietly hope that people from the other party might choose not to vote.

    c) Reluctantly do some research and vote quietly. You're glad when it's over.

d) Read widely about the topics that are important to you, even from sources whose opinions you find offensive, to understand all sides of the debate.

Which of the following best describes how you feel about politics?

a) Frustrated and defeated

b) Lost and nostalgic

c) It's complicated

d) Hopeful

American democracy looks like it is heading in the direction of:

a) Civil war

b) Perpetual unrest

c) A stalemate

d) Healthy compromise

Do you pray for the government or specific government leaders?

a) No, the country is continuing to go downhill.

b) Yes, but only for one political party to win.

c) Occasionally, when you feel despair about the future.

d) Yes, consistently.

You are going to Thanksgiving or another event where you know you'll have to spend a lot of time with people you don't see eye to eye with on politics. How do you prepare?

a) Find a reason to back out. Too much drama and stress.

b) You'll go, but you'll do everything you can to avoid that person or topic.

c) Research and prepare your arguments. Maybe this is the year when you convince your uncle to agree with you.

d) Focus on the time spent together. Some things are more important than politics.

ON HUMILITY

When the presidential political debates are televised, what do you do?

a) Cheer on your candidates and shout down opposing candidates as if you were at a sporting event.

b) Who are you kidding? You're not watching because you know how it ends. You might read a couple of analyses the next day.

c) Pause the debate constantly to fact-check the candidates when they get something wrong and debunk their claims.

d) Try to gather various perspectives on the debate by watching with friends who see things differently or by reading articles from different viewpoints the next day.

Your uncle reposts on Facebook a thread filled with wild conspiracy theories that has been circulating. How do you respond?

a) Get into a debate with your uncle publicly on his post and link articles to your favorite news sites debunking the conspiracy theory.

b) Take a screenshot and send it to a family member or friend with the caption, "Look how crazy this is."

c) Hide your uncle from your Facebook feed so you don't see his posts anymore.

d) Pray for your uncle and maybe ask if he would like to catch up sometime soon.

You are at church when the preacher says something you disagree with politically. What's your reaction?

a) Vow to write the preacher a harsh email on Monday morning to explain your anger that he or she pushed a political agenda from the pulpit.

b) Size up the person beside you quickly and assume they would not be kind to you if you expressed your disagreement.

c) Ask your pastor to grab coffee so you can politely explain your disagreement.

d) Talk with people at your church who are interested in the contentious topic. You hope to foster respect and better understand the other side.

Which adjectives would your family or friends use to describe how you approach political conversations?

a) Aggressive and argumentative

b) Passionate and committed

c) Careful and sympathetic

d) Thoughtful and nuanced

If you were to meet a stranger who held an opposite political belief about a topic you are passionate about, you would feel:

a) Defensive about your own worldview

b) Threatened by their worldview

c) Hesitant to start a conversation

d) Curious to learn more about how they arrived at their beliefs

How often have you changed your opinion on a topic you were confident about?

a) Never

b) Seldom

c) Occasionally

d) I've had to admit I was wrong several times.

Do you believe a Christian can reasonably have a different stance on a controversial issue like immigration reform or gun control?

a) No, not if they've carefully thought through it.

b) On most hot-topic issues there is only one right Christian response.

c) Sometimes, but what really matters is that Scripture is more of a guide than a rulebook for politics.

d) Well-meaning, well-informed godly people can disagree on policy issues.

SCORING YOUR QUESTIONNAIRES

For each set of questions, tally your number of Bs, Cs, and Ds and record them in the blanks.

Then multiply each by the prescribed multiplier (1, 2, or 3) and record the total for each letter.

Finally, add each column of totals and record the score.

HOPE QUIZ		
____BS	MULTIPLIED BY 1	= ____
____CS	MULTIPLIED BY 2	= ____
____DS	MULTIPLIED BY 3	= ____
		HOPE SCORE: ____

HUMILITY QUIZ		
____BS	MULTIPLIED BY 1	= ____
____CS	MULTIPLIED BY 2	= ____
____DS	MULTIPLIED BY 3	= ____
		HUMILITY SCORE: ____

— *Pause here and return to the book (on p. 59)* —

LOCATING YOURSELF ON THE QUADRANT

Look back at your two scores and then locate where you land on the quadrant:

- **Combatant** (15+ hope, 0–15 humility)
- **Cynic** (0–15 hope, 0–15 humility)
- **Exhausted** (0–15 hope, 15+ humility)
- **Disciple** (15+ hope, 15+ humility)

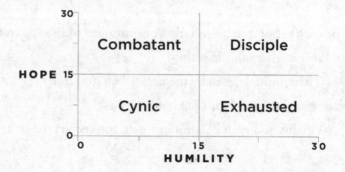

Read the descriptions for each profile. After you read the descriptions, if you scored 15 and 15 or if you do not think the profile you landed in is accurate, choose the one that best describes your posture toward politics.

Note: these profiles are not fixed and you might have different tendencies depending on the discussion topic or your season of life.

THE AFTER PARTY
VIDEO COURSE

✦ ✦ ✦

For more information on the free
After Party video course, go to:

https://redeemingbabel.org/product/the-after-party/

Or scan this QR code:

ABOUT THE
AUTHORS

✦ ✦ ✦

Curtis Chang is the founder and executive director of Redeeming Babel, a ministry that helps Christians make sense of the wider world. He hosts the popular podcast *Good Faith* and is a consulting professor at Duke Divinity School and a senior fellow at Fuller Theological Seminary. He is the author of *The Anxiety Opportunity: How Worry Is the Doorway to Your Best Self* and *Engaging Unbelief: A Captivating Strategy from Augustine and Aquinas*.

Nancy French is a five-time *New York Times* bestselling author, essayist, investigative journalist, and storyteller at the Moth. She has published op-eds and articles in the *Washington Post*, *USA Today*, the *Springfield News-Leader*, *Time*, and other publications too numerous to list. Her investigative journalism into abuse at Kanakuk Kamps appeared on the front page of *USA Today*. She lives in Franklin, Tennessee, and is the author of a new memoir, *Ghosted: An American Story*.

From the Publisher

GREAT BOOKS

ARE EVEN BETTER WHEN THEY'RE SHARED!

Help other readers find this one:

- Post a review at your favorite online bookseller

- Post a picture on a social media account and share why you enjoyed it

- Send a note to a friend who would also love it—or better yet, give them a copy

Thanks for reading!